GROVE PRESS MODERN DRAMATISTS

Grove Press Modern Dramatists
Series Editors: *Bruce King* and *Adele King*

Published titles

Neil Carson, *Arthur Miller*

Ruby Cohn, *New American Dramatists, 1960–1980*

Bernard F. Dukore, *Harold Pinter*

Julian Hilton, *Georg Büchner*

Leonard C. Pronko, *Eugène Labiche and Georges Feydeau*

Theodore Shank, *American Alternative Theater*

Further titles in preparation

NEW AMERICAN DRAMATISTS 1960-1980

by **Ruby Cohn**

Professor of Comparative Drama,
University of California, Davis

Grove Press, Inc., New York

First published 1982 by The Macmillan Press Ltd.,
London and Basingstoke.

First Evergreen Edition 1982
First Printing 1982
ISBN: 0–394–17962–5
Library of Congress Catalog Card Number: 81–84700

Printed in Hong Kong

GROVE PRESS, INC., 196 West Houston Street, New York,
N.Y. 10014

Contents

List of Plates

1. Playwright Neil Simon
2. *Duck Variations* by David Mamet
3. *Alfred Dies* by Israel Horowitz
4. *The Connection* by Jack Gelber
5. *Motel* by Jean-Claude Van Itallie
6. *Bag Lady* by Jean-Claude Van Itallie
7. Playwright Amiri Baraka (LeRoi Jones)
8. *Dutchman* by LeRoi Jones
9. *The Corner* by Ed Bullins
10. *Funnyhouse of a Negro* by Adrienne Kennedy
11. *Bluebeard* by Charles Ludlam
12. *The Moke-Eater* by Kenneth Bernard
13. *Night Club* by Kenneth Bernard
14. *Minnie Mouse and the Tap-Dancing Buddha* by Michael McClure
15. *Pandering to the Masses: A Misrepresentation* by Richard Foreman
16. *The Red Horse Animation* by Lee Breuer
17. Playwright Sam Shepard
18. *The Tooth of Crime* by Sam Shepard
19. *Angel City* by Sam Shepard

vi

Editors' Preface

The *Grove Press Modern Dramatists* is an international series of introductions to major and significant nineteenth and twentieth century dramatists, movements and new forms of drama in Europe, Great Britain, America and new nations such as Nigeria and Trinidad. Besides new studies of great and influential dramatists of the past, the series includes volumes on contemporary authors, recent trends in the theatre and on many dramatists, such as writers of farce, who have created theatre 'classics' while being neglected by literary criticism. The volumes in the series devoted to individual dramatists include a biography, a survey of the plays, and detailed analysis of the most significant plays, along with discussion, where relevant, of the political, social, historical and theatrical context. The authors of the volumes, who are involved with theatre as playwrights, directors, actors, teachers and critics, are concerned with the plays as theatre and discuss such matters as performance, character interpretation and staging, along with themes and contexts.

Editors' Preface

Grove Press Modern Dramatists are written for people interested in modern theatre who prefer concise, intelligent studies of drama and dramatists, without jargon and an excess of footnotes.

BRUCE KING
ADELE KING

To Bill Coco who digs deeper
and with profound gratitude for the teaching theatre of
Herbert Blau
Joseph Chaikin
Joseph Dunn

1
Looking Forward

Lean, blue-jeaned, shaggy-haired, they saunter toward unmarked seats – folding-chairs or backless risers. Here and there an issue of *The Village Voice* bristles out of a jacket pocket, but no one scans the headlines; Vietnam is bombed again, Blacks are arrested again, drugs are discovered again. The light discourages reading, but it is adequate for locating seats near friends, with a view of the uncurtained playing area. The programme is a mimeographed list of credits on cheap coloured paper, easily crumpled to the floor. The same cement floor leads to the playing area on which are arranged – or disarranged – vaguely oval shapes of diverse colours. Desultorily, one by one, actors in leotards approach the ovals, depositing objects behind them. Independently, each actor stretches, twists, gyrates, oblivious of the audience that gradually spreads through the seats. When electronic music sounds faintly, the actors co-ordinate into an arc to perform movements of Tai Chi Chuan. After the closing ceremonial bow, the actors take makeshift costumes from behind the ovals – that's what they were carrying – and put them on. In a procession around the audience, they clap, stamp, whistle, slap their bodies rhythmically. When they have circled back to the playing area, the house lights dim, and the performance begins.

Almost any performance Off-Off-Broadway in the mid-1960s, although the one I describe is fictitious. At the same time, however, professional and amateur actors were presenting plays traditionally in newly built theatres throughout the United States – proscenium, round, or thrust stage, with comfortable seats fixed firmly to carpeted floors. In the mild weather of California, or on balmier days elsewhere, performances took place in parks or on streets. In this country without much theatre tradition, in this technological country with its monstrous film and television industries, there was a sudden burgeoning of live theatre in the 1960s, slowly subsiding during the 1970s, and promising to hold stable during the 1980s.

I can only guess at the causes. Perhaps the behavioural rigidity of President Johnson's U.S.A., Premier Brezhnev's U.S.S.R., and Chairman Mao's China were indirectly responsible. Probably the stereotypical situations and characters of the entertainment industries inspired a widespread reaction against them. From abroad blew fresh theatre breezes murmuring of Artaud and Grotowski, both of whom were rumoured to move performance away from texts and toward the actors, away from developing plots in time and towards filling scenic space. Already in the 1950s the formal dramas of Beckett, Ionesco and Pinter eroded the conception of language as a means of communication; during the 1960s empty political rhetoric further undermined the status of words. In theatre the human body began to speak more convincingly than mere words.

And yet, as soon as I hazard a generalization about the

2

American theatre between 1960 and 1980, I realize that its opposite is also true. Happenings were far less frequent than thoroughly traditional performances. Theatre in the streets and parks was outperformed by theatre in hundreds of new buildings, especially on college campuses. 'Poor' theatres in the wake of Grotowski were countered by the most elaborate technology ever applied to performance. The fluidity of art/life boundaries was opposed by the artifice of strict style. Proliferation of theatre schools contrasted with aggressive amateurs who scorned theatre training. Entertainment-thirsty spectators on expense accounts frequented different theatres from those wooing audience participation. Traditional theatre spectators at first viewed the new theatre as a formless madness, but television soon captured snatches for home consumption. The terminology of theatre reached out to other domains – anthropology, politics, psychology, sociology; to sister arts such as dance, music and sculpture. Mixed media experiments of the 1960s were absorbed by mixed art experiments of the 1970s. Depending on the vantage, one could view the scene as total theatre or total anarchy.

My problem in this volume, then, was selection and organization. My approach to this problem is pedagogical; I have tried to be informative about a broad spectrum of plays. In complementary volumes of this series, Ted Shank and I are led by our individual temperaments – he to describe and photograph Alternative Theatre performances between 1960 and 1980, and I to survey dramatic literature for that period. I examine only those dramatic compositions whose main driving force seems to me verbal, and I omit the mainly visual or musical (performance art on the one hand, and musical comedy on the other). Further, I limit this survey to those dramatists who have produced an available body of work, and by 'available' I mean published. Since I write criticism to stimulate discourse, I feel forced to this arbitrary criterion. Few readers of this book will have seen many contemporary American plays in performance, but I hope to encourage the reading of plays, if only in ephemeral periodicals or (outrageously over-priced) acting editions. (I hope also to encourage perform-ance of some of these plays.)

Although I write in 1980, only a small fraction survives (in print) of the plays performed in the United States during the last two decades. Hundreds of new playwrights were offered performance opportunities in the Off-Off-Broadway fervour of the 1960s and in many new regional theatres. Paradoxically, this easy access to performance was countered by the hard fact that almost no contempor-ary American dramatist could afford to devote full energy to playwriting. Unlike British playwrights, the Americans could not develop the subtleties of their craft by stints in film and television because these American media tend to appeal to the lowest common denominator of response. Nevertheless, dozens of contemporary dramatists have produced a substantial body of plays expressing their deep concerns, while earning a livelihood in other ways.

American dramatists – to flash backwards briefly – have long lived in a situation of quasi-contempt. In the nineteenth century there was no redress against plagiarism; in the twentieth century copyright rarely assured an income. By the mid-twentieth century New York City's Broadway had a stranglehold on the drama market, and, breaking away, Off-Broadway was born in the mid-1950s. (Obie or Off-Broadway awards began in 1956.) Downtown from New York's theatre district in the West Forties (Off-Broadway is, more accurately, off Forties) plays were produced in small theatres before small audiences. In the main these productions were revivals of drama classics or

4

translations of those recent European plays grouped by
Martin Esslin as the Theatre of the Absurd. Few American
dramatists were welcomed Off-Broadway which was traditional in the sense that a dramatist delivered a script to a
director, who then cast the play for rehearsals. Although
revisions might be made, the dramatist published the play
soon after opening – as on Broadway.

Revolt seethed Off-Off-Broadway. Sometimes viewed
as a further step off Broadway, the second 'off' actually
means *against*. Off-Broadway housed low-budget, traditional performances of plays that were intellectually re-
spectable, whether classical or contemporary. Off-Off-
Broadway had no tradition but a rebellious spirit. *The
Off-Off-Broadway Book* of Bruce Mailman and Albert
Poland cites seventeen main performance venues of which
only four are formal theatres. The impetus for Off-Off-
Broadway came from strong personalities in two cafes and
two churches of downtown New York – Joe Cino of Caffe
Cino, Ellen Stewart of Cafe LaMama, the Reverend Al
Carmines of Judson Memorial Church, and Ralph Cook of
St Marks-in-the-Bowrie. These contemporary *Choregi*
welcomed playwrights, performers, audiences in a wide
variety of energetic, inexpensive productions. A high birth
rate and comparable mortality rate typified these under-
takings of the 1960s, where the playwright might function
as a recorder to fix improvised scenes or as an architect to
structure improvised dialogue. The plays did not move
uptown.

It would be a critical convenience if I could pigeonhole
certain playwrights as typically Broadway, others as Off-
Broadway, and still others as Off-Off-Broadway, each
neatly circumscribed in one of my chapters. Inconvenient-
ly, however, playwrights skip or stumble across critical
frontiers, so that it is only by approximation that I assign

certain playwrights – Arthur Kopit, Terrence McNally, Lanford Wilson – to Broadway, and others – Ronald Ribman, David Rabe, John Guare, David Mamet – to Off-Broadway although they have been produced on Broadway. Then my chapters veer away from both groups to more divergent dramatists: playwrights whose work was shaped by acting ensembles; those whose medium was subservient to a message; those who reflected minority experiences; those with an anchor in other arts; and finally Sam Shepard with his impressive *oeuvre*. This organization avoids chaos, but it imposes omissions: Paul Foster and Albert Innaurato who do not quite fit my scheme; Leon Katz, Murray Mednick and Susan Yankowitz who have published too few of their fine theatre explorations; others by inadvertence.

In an invaluable bibliographical survey of American drama, British critic Christopher Bigsby remarks accurately of what I loosely label Off-Off-Broadway: 'This theatre was actually an assault on the notion that art is an artifact produced by a unique sensibility and open to interpretation and evaluation in the conventional sense.' The very nature of theatre prevents its being 'an artifact produced by a unique sensibility', and yet such sensibility has been a formative agent of many theatres of the Western world. I admire such sensibility, and I respond to it as I can, often with 'interpretation and evaluation in the conventional sense'.

At a time when a plethora of words denounces words, in a period when dramas are derogated as 'scripts' and dramatists as 'scriptors', I read a large body of plays as literature which makes sense through words, but also as *dramatic* literature which resonates through words beyond sense. I read these plays sympathetically and critically, commenting in a vocabulary that the playwrights may reject. They have nevertheless been unfailingly generous to me, and I thank them sincerely; I also thank Mark Amitin, Bernard Earley, John Lion, Bonnie Marranca, and Ted Shank for generous indications. I admire the courage and constancy of the dramatists who figure in this book, even when I do not admire particular dramas. Unlike some of these dramatists in the wake of Artaud, I do not believe that metaphysics is absorbed through the skin, but that wisdom can be nurtured through every perceiving sense, including 'the conventional sense'.

2
Broadway Bound: Simon, Kopit, McNally, Wilson

The title of this chapter is an obvious pun. New York's Broadway is both a physical and cultural designation, and for two centuries its drama has enticed theatre audiences who are affluent and entertainment-oriented. The theatre capital of the United States, Broadway is fed by entre- preneurs rather than subsidies, and the dramatist is putty in grasping hands. In his *Seesaw Log* playwright William Gibson offers a disabused description of the playwright as Broadway commodity:

> . . . his work acquires three species of co-workers. The first is in the realm of economics. The producer . . . must be persuaded that accepting the work will not be sheerly an eleemosynary act . . . . The writer here becomes part and parcel of a complex business organization formed to manufacture and sell one article of merchandise . . . . When a producer buys a play it is thus spoken of as 'his' play, and not improperly. The second species is in the sphere of the secondary arts . . . . When a director or

star agrees to do a play it is also spoken of as 'his' play, and not improperly . . . . What is rehearsed is thus several plays . . . everyone wants to make art, and everyone wants to make money, and each goal is confounded with the other. The third species of co-workers is encountered thus in the shape of the be-hemoth-bank which contains the money, and the art becomes that of shaking it out. When a spectator sits to watch a play it is never spoken of as 'his' play, but it properly should be: none of the active hands so tyranni-cally molds the materials as does the behemoth's passive posterior.

Audience as broad-assed behemoth is an unflattering if humorous image to which the durable giants of American drama refused to surrender. Eugene O'Neill, that most serious playwright, launched insidious forays against American progress and optimism. At mid-century two Broadway playwrights were subversive of its habits –Ten-nessee Williams of its sexual practice and Arthur Miller of its social system. More recent Broadway playwrights have sometimes undermined its aesthetic patterns.

Although I mean 'Broadway Bound' as a pun, its bindings were loose on the decreasing number of serious dramas performed between 1960 and 1980. Broadway of the second half of the twentieth century can absorb un-Broadway abrasions on its sunny surface. Most serious Broadway plays, to shift metaphors, sport new tailoring for old garments – family problems à la Robert Anderson, social satire à la Jules Feiffer, suffering loners à la Arthur Laurents, lovable little people à la Paddy Chayefsky or Murray Schisgal. Nevertheless, a few Broadway play-wrights withdrew from box-office formulae, deliberately weakening story line, character motivation, and conclusive finale. Traffic began between Broadway and the avant-garde although the two are by definition mutually exclusive. Through the broadening way, however, the main direction remains family realism, that most illusionistic of theatre styles precisely because it announces its style so minimally.

Today's Broadway playwright, like yesterday's, rarely springs fully formed from some Olympian thigh. Eugene O'Neill was first staged in Provincetown and Arthur Miller at the University of Michigan; Tennessee Williams wrote plays for the St Louis Mummers, and Edward Albee reached Broadway by way of the 1950s phenomenon, Off-Broadway. (These playwrights have books devoted to them in this series.) Unlike younger playwrights, these celebrities were not offered the unparalleled production opportunities of Off-Off-Broadway in the mid-1960s.

Neil Simon, Broadway's most successful playwright, neither knew or needed these opportunities. A television veteran when he turned to drama, Neil Simon might be viewed as a model of Broadway superficiality – stale situations predictably theatricalized within conventional social norms. Although his plays do take that mould, they are not mere computer products. His plays do not melodramatically present a familiar problem to be resolved by the final curtain. Full of one-line quips, his plays expose endemic predicaments rather than soluble puzzles – mismatched couples, misunderstanding generations, rival siblings, bad neighbours, and frail friends. Economically comfortable, his characters are more or less well-meaning blunderers on dead-end roads. 'I like to write about people trapped', Simon has acknowledged, and it is not quite clear whether the traps are manmade or natural, but it is clear that they clamp their victims in hilarious positions. Like the characters of Paddy Chayefsky, Murray Schisgal, and

10

harking back to Clifford Odets, Simon's little people – often Jewish – yearn to be a little bigger or to reach a little further. But Simon's little people are much funnier than their predecessors and have therefore been more profitable to their creator.

Born on 4 July 1927, Neil Simon exemplifies one pattern of Broadway success story – through winning affectionate laughter at familiar characters. A member of New York City's Jewish middle class, Simon is a university graduate who quickly found his niche in industry – the entertainment industry. Young enough to escape service in the Second World War, too old for action in Korea or Vietnam, Simon draws upon the escapist experience of America's urban society. His plays ignore not only wars but also racial violence, drug abuse, energy depletion. Unlike the sourly brilliant Mort Sahl or Dick Gregory, Simon in the 1950s reeled off bland jokes for comedians Sid Caesar, Phil Foster, Jackie Gleason, Jerry Lester, Phil Silvers. When Simon tried drama, his first plots were threads for a string of one-liners indiscriminately delivered by almost all his characters. Yet Simon himself declared: 'The playwright has obligations to fulfill, such as exposition and character building.'

Simon's declaration was a dramatic anachronism by the post-Absurdist 1960s, and he performed his obligation by dissolving his plots into the situations of his central characters. Not until his fourth play did he hit on the title *The Odd Couple*, but it also fits plays written earlier and later in his career. In Simon's *Barefoot in the Park* (1963) Paul, a conservative young businessman, is the mismatched husband of Corie, who indulges in such Bohemian gestures as walking barefoot in the park. By the final curtain there is compromise; each promises to dip into the other's predilections. In *The Odd Couple* (1965), however, the couple remain at odds. Two men of opposite temperaments, rejected by their respective wives, cannot dovetail in a common household, and sloppy Oscar ejects orderly Felix from his apartment. *Last of the Red Hot Lovers* (1969) returns to the accommodation of marriage – after Barney Cashman has figured in odd couples with each of the three women he attempts vainly to seduce. The titular *Gingerbread Lady* (1970), alcoholic Evy Meara, figures in odd couples with her homosexual actor friend, her determinedly ageless girl friend, her brutal lover, and, most importantly, her protective seventeen-year-old daughter. Except for the adolescent girl, these ephemeral couples flail in their traps.

The very title *The Prisoner of Second Avenue* (1972) points to entrapment, and the prisoner's wife describes their expensive cell: 'You live like some kind of a caged animal in a Second Avenue zoo that's too hot in one room, too cold in another, over-charged for a growth on the side of the building they call a terrace that can't support a cactus plant, let alone two human beings.' Chuckles of recognition ripple through any middle-class urban audience. *The Sunshine Boys* (1973) is an ironic title for a pair of retired comedians whose lives have turned to gall and wormwood, but the bitterness is funny. Simon's plays of the 1970s frame sitcom with a very hard edge. Moreover, these plays try to justify their jokes. Through thick and mainly thin of the 1960s, all Simon's characters jab with witty lines, but the jokes of *The Sunshine Boys* spout only from professional comedians, and the lovers of *Chapter Two* (1978) savour each other's quick repartee. At his best, Simon delineates trivial anxieties by means of jokes. Sour or aggressive, paranoid or paradoxical, the one-liners can sketch a landscape of contemporary neurosis.

The Prisoner of Second Avenue is as close as Simon

comes to dramatizing distress, but it is surprising that Broadway's golden boy comes even that close. The play opens on a middle-aged couple, Mel and Edna Edison, at 2.30 a.m., and Simon particularizes the discomforts of night in a Second Avenue apartment – noises, smells, flimsy walls, disfunctioning equipment, and hostile neighbours on all sides. No wonder Mel experiences 'an anxiety attack' even before he loses his job. When the apartment is burglarized, Simon's deft hand milks the consumer losses for comedy. Mel screams: 'I'M HAVING A GOD-DAMNED BREAKDOWN AND THEY DIDN'T EVEN LEAVE ME WITH A PILL TO TAKE!' Out on his terrace, Mel is doused with water by the upstairs neighbour.

By Act II his wife Edna has taken a job to maintain their Second Avenue prison, while Mel sinks more deeply into paranoia. While Edna telephones a psychiatrist, Mel hatches a scheme of revenge against his neighbours; he will douse the water-douser with a shovel full of snow when winter comes. By the last scene Edna has lost her job, and Mel declares himself cured. The Edisons converse in their habitual raucous accusatives. Reversing an earlier scene, Mel comforts an Edna bewildered by *her* loss of job, as by waterless pipes and malfunctioning freezer. When the neighbour again bellows for quiet, Mel goes out on the terrace and is again doused with water, although *his* pipes are waterless. The Second Avenue prisoner-couple sit down exhausted and watch through the window as the snow begins to fall. In the final tableau Mel's 'hand/is/ holding his shovel, the other around Edna's shoulder, a contemporary American Gothic'. Unlike Grant Wood's tableau of American strength, however, Simon's play ends on American neurosis. Mel's shovel will break no ground for plants; it will dump snow on another prisoner of Second Avenue.

Simon implies that America's cities are filled with

prisoners. He does not dramatize the death but the spiritual dearth of an updated salesman, with the fancy title of Advertising Account Executive. Through the device of Roger Keating's newscasts, Simon situates the Second Avenue prison in a city of strikes, crimes, and miscellaneous chaos. Although Simon lacks the large comic imagination for wholesale catastrophe on these broadcasts, he catches the minutiae of urban entrapment. Contemporary American Gothic is consumer urban grotesque. Yet even in this darkest Simon play his Edisons can escape to the country, and other Simon characters are promised the rosier futures preferred by Broadway.

Neil Simon's success is rare on Broadway, and my account neglects his musicals and one-act 'suites', which add to his popularity. For over a decade Simon was produced annually on Broadway, however age may have withered him and staled his infinite stream of one-liners. In contrast is the Broadway career of another native New Yorker of Jewish background – Arthur Kopit with only two plays on the Great White Way. A decade younger than Simon, Kopit saw his first efforts performed while he was still an undergraduate at Harvard University. The early plays add up to a neophyte playwright in search of a style, and two decades later he still lacks a distinctive style. His first play *The Questioning of Nick* (1957) announces his major theme of American corruption. In a single realistic act Nick, a high-school basketball player, is so shrewdly questioned by the police that he confesses to having sold the game. *Sing to Me Through Open Windows (1959)* is a single, vaguely expressionist act loaded with symbols. *Chamber Music* (1962) is set in an insane asylum where each woman patient imagines herself to be a celebrity. After a meeting chaired by someone believing herself to be Susan B. Anthony, the women abandon a plan of attack

against the men's ward and instead lynch one of their own –
a woman believing herself to be Amelia Earhart. Afterwards they prop the corpse at a table, where the asylum
attendants do not even notice she is dead. This drama of a
skirmish avoided at the expense of a life does not violate
realistic surfaces in order to underline a wider theme.

The most substantial of Kopit's early one-acts is *The Day
the Whores Came Out to Play Tennis* (1964) in which he
shifts idiom to Jewish intonations among affluent country
club members coached in English by their butler: 'I've
always *assumed* that my job was to, um, help the members
with their *diction*.' Boldly, and in bold colours, the whores
arrive in garishly painted Rolls Royces to play tennis at the
country club. Their effrontery does not stop at tennis
played without underwear; they fart in unison, they beat a
club member, they pelt the clubhouse with tennis balls, and
they cut the telephone wires. Outraged and incommuni-
cado, the club members retire to the club Nursery to toss
cruel barbs at one another. Disunited, two club members
play cards, another drinks, and a fourth rides a hobby horse
while 'watching what we built collapse all about us'. Under
the theatrical surface, Kopit is of course dramatizing a
wider chaos than that suffered by a country club, as he did
earlier in the asylum cacophony of *Chamber Music*.

Before *Whores*, however, Kopit arrived on Broadway in
1962 (via Cambridge, 1960, and London, 1961) with a title
that soon became the subject of tiresome jokes – *Oh Dad,
Poor Dad, Mamma's Hung You in the Closet and I'm
Feelin' So Sad: A Pseudoclassical Tragifarce in a Bastard
French Tradition*. Both title and subtitle are accurate;
Mamma or Madame Rosepettle carries her husband's
coffined corpse on her travels, and she hangs him in the
closet of any hotel where she stays. This does sadden her
seventeen-year-old son, a stuttering, mother-dominated

Oedipus. The play is farcical in such highjinks as a wooing chase, a near seduction, a corpse falling from a closet, but a tragic note is struck in the violent death – by smothering – of the misguided Rosalie who undertakes the hero's sexual initiation. The 'bastard French tradition' has been analysed by Martin Esslin as Theatre of the Absurd. What neither Kopit's title nor subtitle indicates is the parodic basis of the play; not only Sophocles and the Absurd, but Tennessee Williams, with the Venus fly-traps and piranha fish that recall *And Suddenly Last Summer*, the ubiquitous Rose that recalls *The Rose Tatoo*. Dürrenmatt contributes the imperious millionairess and travelling coffin from *The Visit*. Madame Rosepettle vents her passion in melo-dramatic clichés or the grandiloquent rhetoric of Lady Bracknell, but in the play's final moments she views the assorted corpsed debris and comments as in cabaret comedy: 'As a mother to a son I ask you, *"What is the meaning of this*?" ' Under the parodic surface Kopit addresses that question to his audience, and the answer is easy: sick to its self-indulgent core, modern life erupts in violence. But whereas another Kopit mentor, Ionesco, dramatized the violence as endemic to the human condi-tion, Kopit contrives it capriciously.

The physical exercise of farce nevertheless enabled Kopit to attempt more ambitious scenography in *Indians*, which came to Broadway in 1969 by way of London and the Arena Theatre of Washington D.C.. The book's jacket quotes Kopit's description:

a combination of Wild West Show, vaudeville, and circus . . . . There are dances; phony horses; things go wrong all the time – mock-murders turn into real murders, there are conversations with the dead. It's a hallucinatory mosaic; a nightmare panorama of Buffalo

16

Bill reliving his life and trying to work out where he went wrong.

The main problem is that he doesn't try very hard; he enjoys being a Wild West star.

Indians was successful on Broadway, but two of our most discerning critics differ radically on its quality. John Lahr: '*Indians* is not a protest play, but a process play. With its uniquely American energy, it is both elusive and delightfully specific, a spectacle as well as a haunting vision . . . . *Indians* tackles the gigantic themes of American history and channels them into art.' Elizabeth Hardwick: 'To bring death and vaudeville together we would need a dramatic talent of the highest order . . . . But in this play, with its electronic buffalo stampedes, its restlessly shifting, undeveloped episodes, you feel all about you the old American attitude toward the killing of the Indians: indifference.' By quoting Hardwick last, I vote with her. *Indians* seems to me a spectacular cowboys-and-Indians melodrama updated through a role-reversal in favour of the Indians. Its Broadway success springs from a facile liberalism and an entertaining spectacle. Although faithful to his theme of American corruption as announced in *Chamber Music, Oh Dad,* and *Whores,* Kopit does not probe below the glossy surface of that corruption.

Retreating from the public to the private realm, Kopit did not reach Broadway with *Wings* (1978) but achieved modest success elsewhere. In this play an aphasic ex-aviatrix is lovingly led from a comatose state, through semantic error, to security in the relation of sound to meaning, and into a final verbal aria. (One scene recycles the idioms of *Chamber Music,* written nearly two decades earlier.) Taking command of speech as she had once taken command of her plane, the woman relives her glorious walk out on the wings of a plane in flight.

Wings marks Kopit's graduation in control of theatre language. A decade ago critic Gerald Weales wrote: 'Kopit is still walking the fine line between facility and substance', and he has continued that delicate balance until *Wings*. Married young to the drama, Kopit has been untempted to stray from theatre. But lured by Broadway, he often subdues substance to facility. Only recently has he found a simple form for a simple and absorbing story which does not stumble toward symbolic heights.

The path was somewhat easier for Kopit's Broadway-bound contemporaries who were not produced quite so early. In the late 1960s and during the 1970s they could fall off Broadway's tightrope into other locations than the void. Sometimes a play starts out in another place – notably the annual O'Neill Playwrights' Conference in Waterford, Connecticut, the training camp for Broadway; it is then revised toward the great white lights. Lacking Kopit's ambitious theme of American corruption, Terrence McNally and Lanford Wilson are adroit in bouncing up to Broadway, since both are eclectic in theme and style – McNally more so.

Born in Florida in 1939, McNally was brought up in Texas and educated at Columbia University where he was infected with the Broadway virus. Arthur Ballet, who has encouraged new drama over the years, writes of McNally:

His career is a chronicle of recent American theatrical action – starting off with some ill-fated Broadway productions, removing them to phenomenally successful runs off-Broadway, and eventually into the mainstream of collegiate and regional theatre in the United States. Finally . . . the process is reversing, and a major American dramatist is making his way back to the Big Time.

The 'ill-fated Broadway production' was . . . *And Things That Go Bump in the Night* (1962). Mysterious night-bumps are literally heard toward the end of that play, but more frightening are the *words* of a sadistic family – mother Ruby, her twenty-one-year-old son Sigfrid, her thirteen-year-old daughter Lakme; her father Grandfa and husband Fa cannot hope to compete with the cruel volubility of this trio. Vicious families are not new on Broadway, from O'Neill's Mannons to Hellman's little Foxes, but McNally's family was born into an Absurdist era of obstreperous, expositionless stage presence. The family lives underground, protected by an electric fence, but each night they offer a victim to the powers behind the night-bumps. Act I stages their preparations for a 'guest', and Act II presents him as Clarence, former schoolmate of Sigfrid. In an infernal night Clarence is seduced by Sigfrid and so humiliated by Ruby that he rushes out of the basement and electrocutes himself on the surrounding fence. The family members accuse one another of his death. While the titular bumps (a phrase from a fourteenth-century Scottish prayer) gradually accelerate, Ruby and Grandfa duel for the soul of Sigfrid. When Grandfa is defeated, he slowly climbs the stairs into the night. Mother and children freeze to the sound of Ruby's voice-over, punctuated by the approaching thumps. Cruel and élitist, the family is a remarkably intense creation for a twenty-two-year-old playwright, and . . . *Things* is thereby a remarkably unconventional play for Broadway of the mid-1960s – even for a short run.

McNally's Off-Broadway plays are sometimes extended anecdotes. *Next* (1967), *Tour* (1967), and *Botticelli* (1968) ricochet off the Viet War. Mildly political, too, is *Cuba Si!* (1968) in which an armed woman guerrilla is interviewed by a liberal reporter in New York's Central Park. In their non-meeting of minds, the guerrilla insists that the revolution is near, and the reporter insists just as didactically that America is immune to revolution: 'Cuba is for Cubans and you're a hell of a long way off base as far as anyone in the big leagues is concerned.' Another stab at a political play shares its central image with an unpolitical play; in *Witness* and *Sweet Eros* a human being is gagged and bound. The victim in *Witness* (1969) has been kidnapped on the day of a presidential parade. His abductor mocks a self-righteous window-washer, then a patriotic young lady, but addresses himself mainly to the bound man: 'It'll just be witnessing then right up to the end.' It becomes apparent that the 'end' is assassination of the President. Aiming his rifle from the window, the abductor cries out that marksmen everywhere are shooting at the President. Alone again with his victim, the would-be assassin waves an American flag and signs V for victory – and vapidity?

In *Sweet Eros* (1969) the victim is an auburn-haired young lady, and the play consists of a long monologue by her abductor. Having disgusted his wife with too much love, having driven another woman to suicide because of too little love, the monologuist has kidnapped his victim who has in turn loved another man too much. Coexistence is better than love, evidently, and the abductor teaches his victim to enjoy coexistence – an ironic sweet Eros.

McNally's short plays hazard broad satire, but his most extended effort is *Where Has Tommy Flowers Gone?* (1971). Framed in a musical performance with conductor but no orchestra, *Where Has Tommy Flowers Gone?* is a play within the play, a record played by the Black Stagehand. On stage Tommy Flowers impersonates several contemporary artists – ballerina, musician, actor, opera singer, old lady, young boy, movie star, Marilyn Monroe, teenage seducer, homosexual panhandler, Black activist.

In the semblance of a plot, Tommy teams up with an old actor Ben Delight, a dog Arnold, and a lover Nedda Lemon. Ben dies in a hospital ward, and Nedda is imprisoned in a House of Detention. A man from the audience shoots Tommy (in black face), and he dies with a last call to those he loved. The Black Stagehand asks at the play's end as at its beginning: 'Where has Tommy Flowers gone?' He then explodes bombs that trigger a three-step extinction of lights on Tommy's photo and on the American flag. Tommy Flowers emerges as an American of cheerful, lovable anarchy, who goes the way of some flower children – to a violent death. It is problematical whether meaning would seep through the diffuse flamboyance of performance.

Blander satire marks *Whiskey* (1973) in a Pirandellian frame. Whiskey, a horse television star, is owned by the couple I. W. Harper and Tia Maria. Homosexual Johnny Walker contrasts with Macho Jim Beam and sexually provocative Southern Comfort. Television actors, they are nervous and awkward when they have to appear live before the President in Houston. True to their names, they engage in all-night drinking and are trapped in a fire. Only the horse Whiskey escapes to star in a new televison series, but the old troop, dressed in white and replete with wings, look fondly down at him.

Improbably, two short plays of *Bad Habits* (1974) attained Broadway productions. In *Ravenswood* the bad habits are marital, and wealthy clients go to Ravenswood to learn to live together. In *Dunelawn* the bad habits are self-indulgence, which are cured by no more than a look of reproach from the saintly doctor.

McNally's most successful play is *The Ritz* (1975), a blend of Feydeau and *The Godfather*. Set in a men's bathhouse (euphemism for a homosexual brothel), the play is an excuse for role-switching and caricature. Gaetano Proclo, married to Vivian née Vespucci, is fingered for a 'hit' by her brother Carmine. Proclo arrives at the Ritz, ignorant of its specialization, but he very soon learns about it. He is pursued by Claude the chubby chaser, befriended by the screaming queen Chris, mistaken for his violent brother-in-law by the soprano-voiced heterosexual detective, urged by the bath attendants to impersonate a producer for singer Googie Gomez. In spite of his girth, Proclo moves swiftly not from pillar to post but from near-orgy to near-orgy. Finally, in a Patty Andrews wig, mink coat, dark glasses, and moustache, he is apprehended by his murderous brother-in-law Carmine. The genial bathhouse clients prevent carnage, and Proclo's wife insists upon a kiss of peace between her husband and brother. The play ends as a new orgy starts at the Ritz, with Carmine at its centre.

Fluttering between Broadway and Off-Broadway, McNally illustrates how the former can co-opt bold-looking themes and non-realistic techniques, notably Pirandellian role-playing and broad satire. Co-opting existential anxieties, Neil Simon's characters evoke Broadway laughter. Less anxious and less coherent, Terrence McNally's characters present an unconventional surface; they may utter obscenities, shed their clothes, indulge in sexual deviation, and yet they do so with charm, and without offence. Bound to Broadway, McNally sacrificed the intensity he achieved at the age of twenty-two in . . . *Things*. By the time he was forty, he was manipulating pawns in broad satire.

McNally started on Broadway, fell off, but climbed back on with farcical satire. Lanford Wilson, born in 1937, arrived in New York via Missouri and California, and the three locales provide him with play settings. In the mid-1960s he cut his dramatist's teeth Off-Off-Broadway.

In 1969 he helped found the Off-Broadway Circle Theatre Company and became their main playwright, which proved a stepping-stone to Broadway.

His first plays (1964) reveal kinship with fellow-Missourian Tennessee Williams in plays about unusual sexual situations. Most often performed is *The Madness of Lady Bright,* about an aging homosexual immured in his room among keepsakes and memories. He crosses the border into insanity with much of the bittersweet gentility of Williams' Blanche. A decade before Williams' *Outcry* Wilson wrote *Home Free* about an incestuous couple. Weak and pregnant, a wife/sister for the first time fails to respond to the fantasies of her husband/brother. Her death triggers his madness, and he cradles her corpse with the comfort that they are 'home free'.

Balm in Gilead (1965) is an ironic title, since there is no balm in the play's Gilead, a New York coffee shop peopled by junkies, prostitutes, hustlers and hoods. Wilson etches a sad little love affair in this dead end – of dope dealer Joe and Chicago refugee Darlene. When Joe is knifed for trying to withdraw from drug dealing, Darlene is drawn irresistibly into prostitution. Out of the depths and into the sun moves *The Sand Castle* (1965) named after a California beach house. Sad little love affairs multiply as a daughter seduces her mother's suitor, a son is in love with the pregnant wife of a family friend who tries to seduce another family friend. Like Williams' Tom of *Glass Menagerie,* this son looks back on his past. With the exception of the expressionistic *Wandering* (1967), Wilson's short plays of the 1960s are realistic sketches of sympathetic misfits. In the tradition of Tennessee Williams, Wilson is tender to deviants, valuing them more highly than those who preserve the norms.

In the background of Wilson's plays is an 'Our Town'

where sex drives are repressed, strangers are viewed with suspicion, and no one is allowed to ruffle surfaces. *The Rimers of Eldritch* (1966) dramatizes the evil in the town of Eldritch, with a suspense that is rare for Wilson. Not until a late scene is it clear that a frustrated spinster has shot the town derelict in the act of rescuing a crippled young woman from a sexual assault she provoked. On the false testimony of the crippled woman and her attacker, the murderess is acquitted. The respectable members of Eldritch town, the rimers of Eldritch, close ranks to defend their frozen surface – frozen, too, in a conventional theatre mould.

With *Gingham Dog* (1969) Wilson arrived on Broadway since his misfits were more conventional. His Black Gloria and white Vincent, an ordinary middle-class couple except for colour difference, agree to dissolve their marriage. Although they love one another, the 1960s drive them apart. Wilson's Gloria worries about her Black identity while Vincent is a comfortable cog in a large corporation. Even on Broadway plays can end unhappily. This gingham dog and calico cat do not sleep a wink without one another, and yet they part – implicitly because each is inflexible in a racial attitude. This muted plea for suppleness is the limit of Wilson's politics.

Lemon Sky (1970) returns to a private world. Looking backwards, like the son in *The Sand Castle,* Alan relives events in a family under the lemon sky of California. Foster children complicate erotic attachments, with the protagonist an unappreciated misfit.

Back across the country in Baltimore *HotL Baltimore* (1973) sets a group protagonist in a condemned hotel on Memorial Day: 'The theater, evanescent itself, and for all we do perhaps itself disappearing here, seems the ideal place for the presentation of the impermanence of our

24

architecture', and of its inhabitants. Three prostitutes, one aged nineteen and two aged thirty, are in the tradition of the golden-hearted whore. Other HotL residents are an old man health freak, a spiritualist former waitress, a lesbian health freak and her frail brother. The play consists of interwoven strands of their biographies. By the play's end a transient young man renounces his search for his grandfather, one of the older whores departs to live with a sadistic pimp, and the lesbian abandons her weak brother who is persuaded to dance by the other older whore: 'Come on, they're gonna tear up the dance floor in a minute; the bulldozers are barking at the door.' Wilson means more than a dance floor, and yet his flat language does not urge us to look beyond its immediacy.

With *The Fifth of July* (1978), Wilson embarked on what promises to be a series of plays about the Talley family of Lebanon, Missouri – respectable, intolerant, but sprinkled with Wilson's beloved deviants. The first Talley play opens not on the fifth but the fourth of July, 1977, a symbolic year after the United States Bicentennial. The family members are Aunt Sally, her nephew Ken, whose legs were shot off in Vietnam, his sister June, and her illegitmate daughter Shirley. Visiting the Talleys is not only Ken's lover Jed but also a childhood friend John Landis, his rock-singer wife Gwen, and her composer. The frail plot hangs on Ken's ambivalence about selling the family estate, and Gwen Landis's intermittent desire to buy it. John Landis wants to 'adopt' Shirley, whose father he may be. Indignantly repulsed by June Talley, he leaves, and fourteen-year-old Shirley realises: 'I am the last of the Talleys. And the whole family has just come to nothing at all so far.' But Wilson hints that this family in America's heartland may be pregnant with change; they will keep their land which Ken's lover will teach them to cultivate and which will be nourished by the symbolic ashes of Aunt Sally's Jewish husband Matt.

Talley's Folly (1979) backtracks to Matt on 4 July 1944. The play recounts rather than dramatises the courtship of Sally Talley by Matt Friedman. Like earlier Wilson characters, Matt functions both as narrator and protagonist. Aging misfits, thirty-year-old Missouri Wasp Sally strains against the family code, and forty-two-year-old Jewish Matt has no family or allegiances. Loners, they are attracted to one another, but Wilson delays their union for some hundred minutes of playing time. Talley's Folly puns on the Victorian boathouse setting and Sally's commitment to leave her family so as to share Matt's life. Wilson's forthcoming plays about the Talleys may move forward or backward in a tepid glow of traditional family drama comfortably ensconced – where else? – on Broadway.

Having begun Off-Off-Broadway, Lanford Wilson has steadily increased his characters' charm, making them acceptable in spite of their quirks. Both on and Off-Off-Broadway, he has been the consistent depicter of apolitical, uncommitted deviants. Unlike the stage people of his predecessor Tennessee Williams, Wilson's misfits rarely resort to violence, and they carry no mythic burden.

McNally began on Broadway, Wilson Off-Off, and yet they have negotiated similar trajectories. McNally manoeuvres his figures through the mechanics of farce, whereas Wilson allows a leisurely humour to mellow situations involving misfits, and neither peppers his plays with machine-gun jokes that have brought fame and fortune to Neil Simon. This variety of Broadway surfaces is deceptive, for the form rarely strays from realism – Simon and Wilson – or broad satire – Kopit and McNally. Neither socially nor aesthetically do their plays threaten the loose, vaguely liberal, and mainly affluent Broadway audience.

26

3
Narrower Straits: Ribman, Rabe, Guare, Mamet

In separating 'Broadway Bound' from 'Narrower Straits', I am guided toward the latter by my own impression of playwright's compulsion. Simon alone has kept a stable footing on Broadway, whereas zigzags mark the paths of Kopit, McNally and Wilson. The dramatists of this chapter have executed comparable zigzags, and yet they seem to me further from Broadway conventions in subject and form, but not so far as deliberately to shun the white lights. Each of them has pursued his own bent – Ribman's paradoxical characters, Rabe's obscenity-marked realism, Guare's grotesque wit, Mamet's pithy wit. And somehow they have been lucky enough to get to Broadway in spite of self-consistency.

Ronald Ribman, born in 1932 in New York City and educated through to the doctorate, perseveres in playwriting although he is neither traditional nor avant-garde. Through two decades he remains relentlessly verbal and yet makes no concessions to Broadway. On the surface, he is as eclectic as Kopit, McNally or Wilson, since his plays range over medieval England, Germany in 1955, and contemporary prison and hospital. But searing them all is the theme of man's inhumanity to man. Fortunately for Ribman, Wynn Handman of the American Place Theatre, nominally Off-Off-Broadway, has a taste for verbal playwrights with serious themes, whose characters are caught in credible dilemmas.

Harry, Noon and Night (1964) follows Jewish American Harry, a would-be artist and 'clown of failure', through scenes set in afternoon and night in Munich, 1955. In the first scene Harry pumps an American Army soldier for information about the military establishment, while both men mechanically fondle a prostitute. In the second scene Harry's bourgeois brother arrives in the tawdry room that Harry shares with ascetic German Jewish Immanuel (originally played by Dustin Hoffman). The confrontation of brother and room-mate is a dialogue of the deaf, each claiming Harry for his own milieu. In the final scene Harry returns to the room at night. Even as he listens to Immanuel's account of his brother's visit, he wraps his friend in a mattress and nearly smothers him. When a German neighbour calls out for silence, Harry flings a flowerpot, evidently killing him while he damns the Germans for the holocaust. The police take Harry away, still protesting against German fascism. Immanuel closes the play: 'What about me? Me!' Such open questions will become Ribman's pattern. Jewish-American Harry, a would-be artist with a blind son, a would-be accuser with an uncertain identity, behaves more brutally than the Germans he accuses. Immanuel, the residual European Jew, is caught between an uncaring army and an uncaring American middle class. What about him? Harry, noon or night, offers no answer – victim and increasingly victimizer.

In *The Journey of the Fifth Horse* (1966), Ribman's free

adaptation of Turgenev's *Diary of a Superfluous Man,* he skilfully counterpoints two victims. Against the original story of the spurned lover who dies lonely – a superfluous man – Ribman juxtaposes a publisher's reader who grows increasingly possessed by the diary of the dead lover. The enactment of the diary scenes in the reader's febrile imagination elicits a passionate response from the emotionally starved reader, who is rejected by two women. The fifth unnecessary and suffering horse attached to the doctor's carriage becomes a vivid dramatic metaphor for two superfluous men, the diarist and his reader. And yet the diarist is not finally superfluous because he has spurred the impassioned fantasies of the reader, which we may extend to any reader.

It is unfortunately passion that is lacking in Ribman's peace plea *The Ceremony of Innocence* (1967). Flashbacks show the English King Ethelred resisting his family members and lords in refusing to fight their hereditary enemy, the Danes. The play traces the inflammation toward war of even the most reasonable men of Ethelred's kingdom; his hotheaded son is killed, as is the gentle Danish princess. At the last Ethelred is alone. Distanced from the ongoing Viet War, *Ceremony* was televised without analogies being drawn.

The Poison Tree (1976) decried domestic war within our prisons. A white guard is killed when a Black prisoner reaches through the bars and chokes him. The guard's friend Di Santis is so traumatized by the event, and by the apparent indifference of his fellow-guards, that he hatches diabolical cruelties of his own. By a combination of threat and bribe to a prisoner nearing release date, Di Santis has him conceal a weapon in the mattress of a prisoner about to be paroled. Discovered and charged, that prisoner hangs himself, inflaming the murderous wrath of the other prisoners. After Di Santis taunts them, the guilty victim strangles Di Santis, whom no one lifts a finger to help. Despite a predictable plot, Ribman draws a convincing picture of the prisoners and guards, both brutalized by the system so that no one can live 'by the book'. As the Marxist prisoner explains: 'We are a tall black tree full of poison'. And Ribman catches the languages of several branches of that tree. As in *Harry,* victim is also victimizer, but there are degrees of victimization, and the Black prisoners imply Immanuel's unanswered question: 'What about me? Me!' Again without reply.

Ribman shifts tone sharply in *Cold Storage* (1977), which opened at the American Place Theatre and went on to moderate success on Broadway. The play contains a laugh a minute, but it is black laughter in a hospital conversation between two men suffering from cancer. Armenian Joseph Parmigian, in his mid-sixties, is the more acutely afflicted: 'They took out my bladder, shaved off my prostate, hooked up my large intestine to my urinary tract, and tied my bowels to my hipbone.' Jewish Richard Landau, in his mid-forties, is to undergo exploratory surgery. In their encounter Parmigian is at once witty, cruel, absurd, diabolically pointed as though actually armed with pitchfork. At first Landau pities him, then grows irritated, and then defensive. Through Parmigian's relentless needling, Landau reveals that he alone of all his family escaped from Nazi Germany, when he was a child of eight. Without identity since then, he has never savoured life and can therefore accept a cancerous condition with near indifference, whereas Parmigian clings tenaciously to his residual body. Apprised of this indifference by Parmigian's merciless insight, Landau shares a black joke with the older man, a new sense of life straining through the laughter.

I have made Landau's last laugh sound rosier than it is,

for the play closes on another Ribman open question – whether the two men will sustain courage. During the course of the play, we witness the crumbling of Landau's assurance and the steel centre under Parmigian's frail skin. With Ribman's penchant for open questions and subtle reversals, it is astonishing that he arrived on Broadway at all. (His television plays are simpler in theme and characterization.) The eclecticism of settings and characters might seem to contradict my title of 'Narrower Straits', and yet he is consistent in his presentation of victim/victimizers.

Stylistic rather than thematic consistency marks the work of David Rabe and John Guare. Both have been welcomed by Joe Papp at his Public Theatre, from which he keeps a weather eye out on Broadway. Before meeting Papp, or thinking of theatre, David Rabe (born in 1940 into a middle-class Catholic family) was a university graduate who served in Vietnam. Other playwrights shook heads briefly at the Viet War – McNally in *Botticelli,* Wilson in *Fifth of July,* Guare in *Muzeeka* – but Rabe was actually there: 'And upon return the theater seemed lightweight, all fluff and metaphor, spangle, posture, and glitter crammed into a form as rigid as any machine geared to reproduce the shape of itself endlessly.' Rabe's distaste is more applicable to musical comedy than to drama – even Broadway drama – but it does reflect his impatience with mere entertainment. As a dramatist, Rabe often looked back at Vietnam.

The Basic Training of Pavlo Hummel (1971) traces a soldier's life from basic training to death in Vietnam. Although flashbacks interrupt the plot's linearity, and although a Black surreal companion ruffles the realistic style, the play is basically linear and realistic. European name to the contrary, Pavlo Hummel is an all-American army volunteer, proud of his uniform, profanity, and sexuality. Assigned to the Medical Corps in Vietnam, he

31

has, in Rabe's words, 'romanticized the street-kid tough guy and hopes to find himself in that image'. Hummel requests a transfer to combat duty, where he is twice wounded, but he does not request the home leave to which he is entitled. Ordered again to the front, he goes to a brothel for his habitual prostitute, who is monopolized by a sergeant. Hummel accosts him:

> I don't know who you think this bitch is, Sarge, but I'm gonna fuck her whoever you think she is. I'm gonna take her in behind those curtains and I'm gonna fuck her right side up and then maybe I'm gonna turn her over, get her in her asshole, you understand me? You don't like it you best come in pull me off.

Audiences have savoured this vocabulary, but the sergeant doesn't like it and throws a grenade at Pavlo, who catches it with his bare hands before it explodes. Tough Pavlo takes 'four days thirty-eight minutes' to die, 'and he don't say nothin' to nobody in all that time'. In Pavlo Hummel Rabe has dramatized the basic training of young American males. Only when Pavlo is dying does he reply to the questions of surreal Black Ardell with various intonations of 'Shit', in effect defecating on the Macho code by which he has lived. Hummel's military career, like that of the good soldier Schweik, reflects sardonically on the basic training of his country's army, but Rabe's indictment is at once vague and limited, lacking the maniacal specificity of Kenneth Brown's *Brig* a decade earlier. Pavlo Hummel denies being a victim, animal, fool, but the play as a whole denies his denial.

Sticks and Bones (also 1971), more sentimental and broadly satiric, was successful on Broadway where it won the Tony Award over Simon's *Prisoner of Second Avenue*.

As Simon's Edisons are prisoners of Second Avenue, Rabe's Nelsons are prisoners of their cheery middle-class home. Easy clichés are the order of their day, an order that is violated when Vietnam veteran David returns to his family – blind. Lifted from a long-running television series, the family – father Ozzie, mother Harriet, brother Ricky – refuse to recognize David's affliction, both physical and psychological. (David Rabe's protagonist carries his own name.) *Sticks and Bones* wavers uncertainly between broad satire of an all-American sitcom family and the realistic suffering of blind, misunderstood David. Rabe has commented: 'Though /the family/ look right at things, though they listen closely, they do not see or hear.' On stage, however, they do little looking or listening, and they are compelled to notice David, who longs for the Vietnamese prostitute he keeps addressing in his fantasy. David proves to be such a threat to his family's well-being that they urge him to slit his wrists with his brother's razor: 'Harriet has brought silver pans and towels with roosters on them. The towels cover the arms of the chair and David's lap. The pans will catch the blood. All has been neatly placed.' Too neatly for credibility in a realistic play, although acceptable in broad satire. *Sticks and Bones* is apparently named after the street rhyme: 'Sticks and stones can break my bones,/ But names can never harm me.' Rabe has tried to stage the harm of sticks, stones, *and* names.

In his next play Rabe aimed at a more positive hero and fell flat on his pen. *The Orphan* (1973) dramatizes *The Oresteia,* with intercuts of a Manson-type family and recollections of My Lai brutality. After the straightforward plots of Rabe's first two plays, and despite a surrealistic non-white in each, Rabe reaches for myth. He invents a Figure who is sometimes Apollo and sometimes Calchas; a Speaker who situates the story in a cosmic context; two identically dressed Clytemnestras, ten years apart in age; a sententious Chorus. Long passages of Rabe's prose occasionally dissolve into embarrassing efforts at verse, and the whole is tedious confusion.

Leaving Vietnam, only obliquely the setting of *The Orphan*, Rabe rather surprisingly wrote *The Boom Boom Room* (1974) which was greeted as a feminist play. Its protagonist Chrissy is the obverse of Pavlo Hummel. As he progresses from army victim to tough guy who is an unknowing victim in an unjust war, she progresses from family victim to socially aware victim in a male-dominated society. As a dying Pavlo intones 'Shit' to all he has lived by, Chrissy wears a mask when she dances topless, hiding the gullible face that reflected her life.

In the play's first scene Chrissy's father nostalgically recalls beating her with a strap, and just before the last scene Chrissy's husband beats her to crush her incipient independence. Father, mother, lover, gay friends of both sexes, and, finally, husband martyrize Chrissy; her very name is a Christ-derivative. Like Rabe's Hummel, Chrissy contributes to her own downfall, but her frailties are dwarfed by comparison with those of society. More aware than Hummel, she dons the self-obliterating mask. The Boom Boom Room, a sexual marketplace, is Rabe's metaphor for contemporary American civilization, where art degenerates to pandering. It is a resonant image, but Rabe lacks the language to render it deeply. Chrissy's lines are flat and abstract: ' . . . people'll never be happy livin' the way I have. I mean, cruel and mean and selfish. When I didn't even have a self in me.' The *word* 'self' is an insuperable obstacle for dramatizing the self.

Rebounding from feminism, Rabe produced *Streamers* (1976), more truly than *The Orphan* his third Vietnam play. Copyrighted as *Knives* in 1970, frankly realistic, it is

Rabe's least pretentious and most coherent play, accommodating a multiple protagonist – three occupants of an army Cadre room. The title comes from the song of the paratroopers: 'Beautiful Steamer/ Open for me'. Yet the original title *Knives* relates more explicitly to Rabe's action. At play's start Martin has cut his wrist in an attempted suicide, but he is saved by his Cadre-mate Richie. At the play's end homosexual Richie's enticements have resulted in the stabbing of his Cadre-mate Billy and his Sergeant Rooney.

Black Roger and educated Billy are willing soldiers; Richie flaunts his charms at Billy. Into the room come two kinds of outsiders, two drunk old sergeants soon to leave for Vietnam and rootless Black Carlyle. When Carlyle commandeers the room for fornication with Richie, Billy taunts him. Anger flares, Billy insulting Carlyle's race and Carlyle insulting Billy's education. In the mêlée no one is sure of who is wounded or how seriously. When drunk Sergeant Rooney staggers in, Carlyle stabs him. After the bodies of Billy and Rooney are removed, Black Roger and homosexual Richie are joined by Sergeant Cookes, ignorant of the deadly events. He tells of his own drunken evening that has resulted in several traffic deaths; he rambles on about his pointless murder of an old Vietnamese man. In nonsense syllables, the old doomed Sergeant sings the melody of 'Beautiful Steamer' and then imitates an explosion: 'He begins with an angry, mocking energy that slowly becomes a dream, a lullaby, a farewell, a lament.'

Except that Rabe's pace is never slow, the scenic description fits Rabe's whole theatre version of the American Army in the 1970s. Although *Sticks and Bones* is the only Rabe play to reach Broadway, his conventions can be accommodated there – specific milieu realistically reflected, coherent characters caught up in violent events, profanity and sexuality commensurate with the army ambience. It is only his seriousness that might offend on Broadway, so that Rabe remains at its boundary at Papp's Public Theatre.

Seriousness is not readily associated with John Guare. Born in New York City in 1938, given a conventional middle-class Catholic education, Guare began unconventionally at the age of ten to write plays, but none was produced until he was a graduate student at Yale University. An enlistment in the Air Force interrupted Guare's writing. While labouring over *House of Blue Leaves* (which took him five years to complete, after some ten revisions) Guare had two short plays produced Off-Off-Broadway at Caffe Cino in 1966. A year later *Muzeeka* was performed, first at the O'Neill Foundation and then at the Los Angeles Mark Taper Forum.

Muzeeka shows Guare's inventiveness and facility. Unrealistic monologues alternate with direct address to the audience as violence erupts out of domesticity. The titular Muzeeka is the canned music of conformism, which overtakes Jack Argue (whose name is an anagram of Guare). Although inspired by the Dionysian dances of the Etruscans, Argue becomes a junior executive for Muzeeka, marries a nice girl, has a suburban house and a baby. On the night his baby is born, he goes to a whore in Greenwich Village for a 'Chinese basket job'. Glad to be drafted, Argue is soon in Vietnam, where the soldiers fight for television coverage of their skirmishes. When his soldier buddy offers Argue a share in his father's business and marriage to his sister, Argue stabs himself. At home his wife intones patriotic platitudes, the Greenwich Village whore intones hip platitudes, his Vietnam army buddy intones military platitudes, and a stagehand pours the ketchup of Argue's blood.

After this dry run Guare in 1969 was ready for Broadway, which he misjudged to the tune of two one-act plays, instead of the conventional one play per evening. *Cop-Out* exercises an actor and an actress in a series of roles that parody televison types. The true-blue Cop (whose first baby word was 'Lease-Po') falls in love with the true-red radical. In a sub-plot super-sleuth Brett, aided by a *femme fatale*, solves a parody murder mystery. After a series of transformations that deflate American celebrities, the *femme fatale* dies in Brett's arms, and he resolves to 'get all you Commie Jewo Niggo Dago Woppo Mafio Faggo Russki'. The amorous Cop, whose vasectomy seals off his love for the hippie striker, shoots her when she insists on picketing. She lies in the aisle while the audience files out. In contrast to this parody of contemporary politics, *Home Fires* (on the same Broadway bill) is set in 1918, the night after the First World War armistice is signed. The play shows that 'home fires' are stoked by runaway servants and immigrants who deny their origin. The plays rambled to a Broadway halt within a week.

Devastated at this failure, Guare fled to Europe and returned in 1970 with *The House of Blue Leaves*. He himself designated it as a marriage of Feydeau and Strindberg, or a painful domestic situation played as farce. The House of Blue Leaves is an insane asylum, and the inhabitants of a Queens, New York apartment convert it to an insane asylum when they step in and out of three doors and a window. The spirited cast is comprised of Artie Shaughnessy, zoo-keeper and failed song-writer, his mad wife Bananas, his culinary mistress Bunny, his AWOL son Ronnie, his movie-producer friend Billy Einhorn, *his* deaf girlfriend movie star, three nuns, and a policeman. The meeting of these faithful Catholics occurs on the day the

Pope visits the United States, and the sidewalks of Queens are lined with worshippers. The ex-altar-boy AWOL son wishes to assassinate the Pope with a homemade bomb, but when seized by a policeman, he tosses the bomb to the movie star. The ensuing explosion kills her and two of the three nuns. Bereft Billy makes off with Artie's mistress, and an abandoned Artie tenderly strangles his wife. In marrying Feydeau of the precipitous doors to Strindberg of the restraining straitjacket, Guare complained: 'Who says I have to be confined and show a guy slipping on a banana peel? Why can't I take him to the next level and show him howling with pain because he's broken his ass?' Guare hasn't learned the simple answer: because a broken ass on stage is funny, and the audience will not believe the pain.

By 1972 Guare did not have to think of pain. Not only did *Blue Leaves* win an Obie and the New York Drama Critics Circle award, but also his adaptation of *Two Gentlemen of Verona* (with music by Galt MacDermott) was voted the best musical. Rich and rather famous, Guare wrote *Rich and Famous* about a Broadway playwright with the farcical name of Bing Ringling. One actor plays Bing, and another plays all other male parts, while an actress plays all female parts. On the opening night of Bing's first produced play – but the 843rd he has written – we are flashed back through scenes that resulted in this gala event. At the play's start, Bing appears in full dress with new cuff-links initialled 'R' and 'F' for rich and famous. By the play's end, having understood the sordid seductions of Broadway, Bing takes off one cuff-link and throws it away. Dressed exactly like him, so do the actor and actress. Bing then tries to remove the other cuff-link, but it won't come off. 'He can't give up that final cuff-link. He lowers his hands in dismay. The other two follow suit.' In performance, the cuff-link did come off, but the acting script is sourer.

Landscape of the Body (1977) parodies another aspect of New York City, but Guare sees the play as 'people fighting against the death in all our lives'. Death is grisly soon after the opening scene in which a disguised passenger on the Hyannisport–Nantucket ferry apprehends a woman for beheading her adolescent son. Flashbacks present the woman, Betty, arriving with her son Bert in Greenwich Village to bring her sister Rosalie back to the wholesome life of Bangor, Maine. Run over by a low-speed bicycle, Rosalie is killed, but she reappears to sing and inspire Betty who 'stays in New York to settle /her sister's/ estate along with /her/ hash'. While Betty works, her son Bert lures homosexuals to their apartment, where his friend Donny robs and kills them. Interrupting the promising New York careers of the down-Maine mother and her son comes Durwood Peach to lure Betty to the South. Mad, he is committed by his family to an asylum, and Betty returns to New York where her son Bert was robbed and beheaded by his friend Donny. In grief, Betty travels as far as her slender resources permit – to the ferry. There the detective offers Betty his love which, after *sotto voce* advice from dead sister Rosalie, she mutely accepts, and Guare apparently believes that all's well that ends well.

Even more diffuse and self-indulgent is *Marco Polo Sings a Solo* (1977). Far from the Italian Renaissance, the play is set in Norway in 1999 where Stony McBride is making a movie about Marco Polo. Sexual and professional cross-couplings explode into intergalactic chaos. From outer space, Stony lyricizes: 'I want no more solos. I crave duets. The joy of a trio. The harmony of a quartet. The totality of an orchestra. Home.' Stony is reborn as his son, but the loquacious characters nevertheless sing their solos before he returns to little old Earth.

After these sallies Off-Broadway, Guare returned to

Broadway with the small cast, reined fantasy, but unsub-
dued wit of *Bosoms and Neglect* (1980). His most skilfully
constructed plot – a prologue and two acts on three realistic
sets – and clearly delineated characters were soon swept off
the Great White Way, but they have graced several other
theatres in the very year of opening.

In the Prologue forty-year-old Scooper learns that his
blind, eighty-three-year-old mother has cancer of the breast
– in her euphemism 'bosom': 'Bosoms are fun. Bosoms are
round.' Act I is a long witty duet between Scooper and
beautiful Deirdre, who have for months been prowling
around one another, since they go to the same psycho-
analyst. Each has been suffering from neglect –
Deirdre by her father and husband, Scooper in a recurrent
dream. Through their respective biographies, they play
witty games about neglected writers. Since they are psycho-
logically damaged people whose psychiatrist is leaving
town, they close the act violently: 'They punch each other.
They stab each other. They are weeping and biting and
attacking each other.'

Act II takes place in the hospital room of Scooper's
mother. The operation is more or less successful, but the
patient is doomed. Nevertheless, Scooper's mother
vituperatively rejects his suggestions of suicide by sleeping
pills. Into the room hobbles Deirdre on crutches, and
Scooper follows her into the outer world while his blind
mother, unaware of his departure, confesses the event
which he has been reliving in nightmares. Confession
ended, she reaches for his absent hand, uttering the
traditional wish of Broadway mothers: 'A better life for
you.'

Like Neil Simon, John Guare endows his characters with
wit at the expense of credibility. Tending to self-indulgence
at the expense of drama, Guare seems most recently to be

in control of wit and farce. In *The House of Blue Leaves* we were barely introduced to Guare's Strindbergian characters before they were slammed by Feydeauian doors. A decade later farce simmers down to neurosis in *Bosoms and Neglect,* and the Strindbergian note sounds only in a loveless mother–son family, a loveless daughter–father (offstage) family. True to Broadway desire, a new couple finally forms, and yet the coupling bristles with psychological peril. The contemporary avatar of happy endings is person-to-person warmth, however fragile, however improbable. Sentimentality has a new hard edge.

That description also fits a younger playwright, David Mamet, born in Chicago in 1948. Preoccupied with the problematics of personal relations, Mamet conveys them in the most economical dialogue of the 1970s. At the age of twenty-three, in *Duck Variations* (1971), he showed mastery of the speech of old men – rambling, repetitive, pugnacious. As in Albee's *Zoo Story* a decade earlier, two men meet on a park bench. As in the Theatre of the Absurd, Mamet's two men are totally concentrated in their stage presence. In *Zoo Story* Albee endows Jerry and Peter with a wealth of expository information, but Mamet reveals next to nothing about his Emil Varec and George S. Aronovitz; even their names go unuttered in the dialogue.

In a park at the edge of a lake 'two gentlemen in their sixties' pass a spring afternoon. They savour their surroundings, particularly the ducks on the lake. No simple metaphor for man, the duck grows progressively more human through the imaginative old men. Early in their conversation, we hear:

> GEORGE: Ducks like to go . . .
> EMIL: . . . yes?
> GEORGE: Where it's *nice* . . .

41

even as old men go to a lake in spring. George opens the next 'variation' with a poignant but pithy generalization: 'You know, the duck's life is not all hearts and flowers.' Subsequent 'variations' circle around the specifics of a duck's life – their troubles, loneliness, exotic breeds, migrations, societies, dangers. In the thirteenth 'variation' histrionic George imagines a hunter stalking a duck, and then describes the heroic death of the bird. It is Emil, however, who dominates the final 'variation', conjuring centuries of bird-watchers, from the ancient Greeks on: ' A fitting end./To some very noble creatures of the sky./And a lotta Greeks.' At once funny and sad, vivid and visionary, *Duck Variations* includes its own epitaph: 'A crumbling civilization and they're out in the Park looking at birds.' In the theatre, however, they're out on stage *talking* about birds – in a brilliantly stylized idiom.

Sexual Perversity in Chicago opened in Chicago in 1974, played Off-Off-Broadway in 1975, and Off-Broadway in 1976. The single act comprises thirty-four variations on the theme of sex. The four characters – two young men and two young women – are obsessed with sex, an obsession they express in careless obscenities and formulaic intimacies. In the first scene, set in a singles bar, two young males talk about sex; the elder of the two, Bernard Litko, describes an unusual encounter to his friend Danny Shapiro. Some nine weeks later, on a beach, the same two friends ogle female bodies. During the summer Dan and Deb have fallen in love, lived together, and separated. Their brief union has been marred by the callousness of Bernie toward Deb, by the hostility to Dan of Debi's friend, Joan. When Deb returns to the flat she shared with Joan, she admits her own fault. On the beach, neither young stud mentions Deb. When an attractive (but invisible) woman does not respond to their greeting, Danny explodes: 'Deaf *Bitch*', venting his frustration at what he has lost.

The 'sexual perversity' of the title is a refusal to invest sexual relations with affection. Structured in swift scenes that rise like dirty jokes to punch-lines, the play is almost barren of setting although it moves through bars, offices, dwellings and a beach. These nominal locales are sounding-boards for sexuality. The cult of the cool governs human relations. As the conversation of *Duck Variations* reveals the fundamental loneliness of two old men, so the conversation of *Sexual Perversity* reveals the fundamental emptiness of four young people. And to each Mamet supplies an accurate idiom.

The idiom changes in *American Buffalo,* which arrived on Broadway in 1977. Conversation is again front and centre, although the characters are petty hoodlums. Mamet achieves freshness even in tough talk: 'Only, and I'm not, I don't think, casting anything on anyone; from the mouth of Southern bulldyke asshole ingrate of a vicious nowhere cunt can this trash come.' The American buffalo is the buffalo-headed nickel found in Don's junkshop, which inspires a fantasy crime against its purchaser – a crime masterminded by Don for performance by Bob. When Teach appears in Don's shop, he convinces the latter to let him replace Bob in the action. Near midnight, when the robbery is scheduled, Bob appears with another buffalo nickel. His presence embarrasses Don and irritates Teach, who hits the young man. Bob confesses that *he* bought the valuable nickel, invented the rich coin-collector, and suggested the burglary. In frustration, Teach trashes Don's shop and then, subdued, he prepares to take Bob to the hospital for his injured ear – the ear that Teach injured. Don then apologizes to Bob, and Bob to Don who assures him that he 'did real good'. American buffalo is human as well as nickel in the tough talk that 'buffaloes' the meek, who inherit nothing.

Like *American Buffalo, A Life in the Theatre* (1977) opened Off-Broadway and then moved uptown. This play too circles round to its beginning. After a performance an older actor and a younger actor exchange 'Goodnights' and then leave the theatre in first and last scenes. In the first scene, however, young John is deferential to experienced Robert; by the last scene, John is better known and borrows money from Robert who, alone, murmurs: 'The lights dim. Each to his own home.' But their true home is the theatre, which Mamet dramatizes in skilful vignettes of hackneyed Broadway or Hollywood acting vehicles – in the trenches, in Elizabethan garb, caught in adultery, in death throes, in a lifeboat, in the surgery; through these scenes thread missed cues, forgotten lines, broken props, against the steady slope of a rising younger actor and a falling older one. Mamet's infallible ear captures the careless artifice and the offstage rhetoric of Broadway professionals in a life as superficial as their calling, and yet Mamet fails to intimate that superficiality rather than nostalgia for the good old scenes.

As *A Life in the Theatre* revives old theatre scenes, *The Water Engine* (1977) revives old radio. A 1930s radio play is set in a 1970s studio; the inventor of an engine that will run on water is assassinated by vested interests threatened by the invention. Interrupting this play of another era are announcements about chain letters, snatches of 1930s music, barkers for the 1934 Chicago World's Fair. The play gently mocks a World's Fair predicting a century of progress, while the inventor of an ecological miracle is annihilated.

Reunion (1977) turns back from the social to the personal; it ends, as the title implies, in person-to-person warmth. A fifty-three-year-old father has a reunion with his twenty-five-year-old daughter whom he abandoned years ago. In contrast to *Duck Variations,* lacking all exposition, *Reunion* consists almost wholly of delayed exposition; father has had several jobs, several women, too much alcohol. Daughter is married to and working for an older man with two children. Finally, father presents daughter with a bracelet, and they go to dinner together, loneliness assuaged – for the time being.

The Woods (1977) is Mamet's most searching play to date. The title is almost Dantean – in the middle of a life, self-discovery in a dark wood. Mamet dramatizes the middle of a love affair, with self-discovery in a run-down summer house near the woods. Nick and Ruth, city lovers, go there to be alone. The house belongs to Nick, and urbanite Ruth is determined to relish the country flora, fauna, and atmosphere. She relishes loquaciously, recalling her grandmother, whose bracelet she has lost. Nervous Nick thinks of his father, who spent a night during the Second World War in a fox hole with a madman who later visited the family in this very house. Though each member of the couple repeats 'Tell me', they are self-absorbed. Late night finds them passionless. Nick is unable to sleep, and Ruth is ineffectual in comforting him, although she tries to tell him one of her grandmother's stories about being lost in the woods. During a storm, they drink, quarrel, revert to recollections of father and grandmother. Their rapport is at a low point when Ruth gives Nick a bracelet inscribed with her eternal love. In the morning their nerves are raw, and Ruth has packed to leave. Their quarrel explodes into violence, with Nick on the verge of madness. Yet they finally cling together, and Ruth again tries to comfort Nick with her grandmother's story of two children lost in the woods. Both in and outside the story, it is not at all certain that comfort is attained, for Mamet subdues our laughter at his characters in order to delineate a loneliness that can be assuaged only momentarily.

David Mamet creates the most concentrated American stage speech since Edward Albee, and it was Albee who remarked that Mamet had a fine ear, but there was as yet no evidence of a fine mind. 'Fine', however, is just what I do call Mamet's mind, in the sense that T. S. Eliot wrote of Henry James' mind – so fine that no idea could violate it. Virtually bare of ideas, Mamet's mind functions through words – repeating, inverting, clipping phrases, pacing short exchanges with arbitrary 'Yeses' and 'Noes' – woven into tapestries of lonely people in brief tense scenes. From *Duck Variations* to *The Woods* Mamet creates characters who are not wisecrackers like those of Simon or Guare. Not witty themselves, they figure in scenes of Mamet's wit. In the second half-century's tradition of lovable little people, they speak more deftly than their contemporaries. Confined to clipped scenes, they reveal no depths. Brevity and private lives are at once Mamet's strengths and weaknesses.

The playwrights of this chapter are in the dire straits of fame and fortune. Each with more substained originality than those who aim for Broadway's blandishments, they nevertheless are imperilled. Ribman's recent plays stretch toward relevance. Rabe's reaction against Broadway pushes him at times to pretentious symbolism or facile satire. Guare's quick wit and farcical physics are so readily rewarded on Broadway that he betrays his Strindbergian intention. Mamet's frugal phrases accumulating in tense scenes are too often suffused in a sunset glow. These playwrights are brave enough to follow their markedly individual ways, skilful enough to create characters that compel attention. Perhaps it is unreasonable to demand *whole* plays.

4
Actor Activated: Gelber, Horovitz, Van Itallie, Terry, Fornès

Broadway, Off-Broadway, Off-Off-Broadway are only approximations, and I have indicated crossovers. This chapter will be purer, and yet not wholly pure in its survey of playwrights who were closely involved with performance. Even then, I limit myself to those with a corpus of plays in print. (Regrettably, I omit Leon Katz and Murray Mednick, whose *Making of Americans* and *Hawk*, respectively, are among my most vivid impressions of Off-Off-Broadway, but neither writer has published enough.)

In 1957 Julian Beck and Judith Malina found a home for their Living Theatre. At Fourteenth Street and Sixth Avenue in New York City, this building was not only off the Broadway theatre district in the mid-Forties, it was not a theatre at all but a disaffected department store. Working swiftly, volunteers converted it to theatre space, seating 160. Even though the conversion broke into the minimal prose-for-photographs of *Life Magazine*, this birth of Off-Off-Broadway was no signal for cigars and champagne, and baptism did not occur until 1960, by reviewer Jerry

47

Thalmer in *The Village Voice*. The Becks opened their theatre with *The Connection* by Jack Gelber, who had carried the manuscript to them personally because he could not afford to mail it. The twenty-six-year-old author assumed that only the adventurous Living Theatre could be receptive to his radical subject. Julian Beck later recalled:

> I read some passages at random as I always do, then took it to Judith's room and told her that I thought we had to do it. It's a funny thing, but *The Connection* and *The Brig* were the two plays that made a splash, and we decided to do them both the very day we received each of the scripts.

With the serendipity that has sustained the Becks through adversity, they chose the play that became a clarion call for the theatre of the 1960s, thriving as it did on drug indulgence, racial commingling, group improvisation, and erosion of barriers between actors and audience. Set in a makeshift room with homemade furniture, *The Connection* was staged for $900 at a time when an Off-Broadway production cost $15,000, and Broadway costs for a non-musical mounted toward $100,000. Living Theatre actor Pierre Biner summarizes their shock technique: 'Make-believe and reality were deliberately blended by Judith during intermission, when the actors mingled with the audience, asking for a fix in the characteristic tone and manner of addicts.' The daily press was outraged, one review dismissing *The Connection* as 'a farrago of dirt, small time philosophy, empty talk and extended runs of cool music'. Reviewers on quality weeklies, however, were enthusiastic, notably Robert Brustein, Henry Hewes, and Kenneth Tynan. The play filled the house for some three years (not continuously), and Shirley Clarke filmed an edited version. It was revived Off-Broadway in 1980, after many productions throughout the country.

The jazz improvisations in *The Connection* and an illusion of verbal improvisation spurred the Becks to actual improvisation in the aleatory plays of Jackson MacLow. The Living Theatre produced only two more fully scripted plays (their twenty-eighth and twenty-ninth) – Jack Gelber's *Apple* (1961) and Kenneth Brown's *Brig* (1963). The latter, with its relentless repetition of United States Marine Corps drill, initiates the audience-assault technique associated with the Living Theatre as international wanderers. Their *hejira* was triggered by the United States Internal Revenue Department when its agents closed the Fourteenth Street building in October, 1963 – for nonpayment of taxes.

Before this event, the company's most gifted actor, Joe Chaikin, founded another company, the Open Theatre, to open the actor to his craft and to the audience. At first conceived as a laboratory to explore non-naturalistic (and therefore non-Method) acting, the Open Theatre worked with several playwrights during its decade of existence, notably Jean-Claude Van Itallie and Megan Terry. In 1959 Joe Cino had opened his cafe to anyone who wanted to do theatre, and in 1961 poet Joel Oppenheimer's *Great American Desert* played at the Judson Memorial Church, directed by Living Theatre alumnus Lawrence Kornfeld. Even before the Becks left for Europe in 1963, cafe and church welcomed theatre, and by the end of the 1960s hundreds of pieces were performed by over a hundred new playwrights in unorthodox spaces. A minority continued to write when the swinging 1960s stiffened into the more restrictive 1970s. In a review of *The Off-Off-Broadway Book* Lanford Wilson laments the dearth of publication of playwrights of that effervescent decade, mentioning Julie Bovasso, Donald Dvares, Robert Heide, Corinne Jacker,

H. M. Koutoukas, Roy London, Claris Nelson, David Starkweather, Arthur Williams, Jeff Weiss, Doric Wilson; four of these are published in the *Book*, as well as others unmentioned by Wilson. Despite omissions, however, a corpus of 1960s plays *has* been published in a flurry of paperback anthologies. Usually economical to stage, these plays thumb noses at the realistic illusions of Broadway and Hollywood; their authors were more or less committed to a raucous avant-garde. Although they might be personally political, they dramatized social issues only obliquely, if at all. Receptive to other arts – music, film, sculpture – these playwrights defied literature to concentrate on performance.

The Connection was the trumpet of the Off-Off-Broadway movement, with its disaffiliation and audience infiltration. Like many of the disaffiliated of the 1960s, Gelber was a university graduate who knew his Pirandello. *The Connection* presents fictional director and author, as well as two cameramen to observe characters who are not in search of an author, but who are hoping for a fix. In the first two acts the drug addicts await the arrival of Cowboy, who has gone to obtain 'horse' (heroin) from 'the connection' (supplier). One of the junkies spells out the play's metaphor: '. . . the chlorophyll addicts, the aspirin addicts, the vitamin addicts, those people are hooked worse than me'. Gelber views us as hooked and waiting for a connection, as a decade earlier Beckett had viewed us all as waiting for Godot. Unlike Godot, Cowboy does arrive – in Gelber's Act II.

In print *The Connection* is a melodrama on a subject that was bold at the time. Among Gelber's junkies are good guys (Sam, Solly, the jazz musicians) and bad guys (Ernie and Leach). A rising action is climaxed first by the arrival of Cowboy and then by Leach's overdose of heroin (at which

spectators fainted in the original production). Conventional comic relief comes from the *naïveté* of a Salvation Army
sister. The play ends happily, with everyone getting his fix,
and the fictional playwright remarks: 'We wouldn't all be
on the stage if it didn't fit.' Fit it does, very neatly indeed,
although it was considered free in 1959.

What was radical, aside from the subject, racial mixture,
and improvisational effect, was Judith Malina's direction.
Shirley Clarke filmed a well-made play, but in the original
stage version Malina alternated monologues with jazz riffs,
rejecting suspense and disorienting the audience. Peter
Brook wrote in *Encore* in 1960:

> In twenty years, *The Connection* will seem plot-ridden
> and contrived . . . . *The Connection* proves to me that the
> development of the tradition of naturalism will be
> towards an ever greater focus on the person or the
> people, and an increasing ability to dispense with such
> props to our interest as story and dialogue.

Perhaps Brook should be hailed as a prophet as well as a
director.

Gelber himself apparently wished to dispense with such
props as story if not dialogue, and in his next play *The
Apple* (1961) he minimized plot but exploited the device of
Pirandellian play, fascinated as he was by Living Theatre
actors. Gelber sets on stage six actors instructed to use their
actual names and not those in the text. They will improvise
a show in a restaurant. In charge for the evening is Anna,
an Oriental-American, with Black Ace functioning like a
Stage Manager. Gelber offers no motive for staging this
show, which lacks the political and racial pressure of the
ritual–ceremony in Genet's *Blacks*, playing Off-Broadway
at this time. Rather than Genet's rape/murder of white by

Black, Gelber's actors utter banal dialogue in stereotypical domestic scenes.

As *The Connection's* action rose to the entrance of Cowboy, *The Apple*'s action rises to the exit of vicious Tom. Gelber supplies visual analogues of *The Connection*'s jazz in mannequins, action painting, animal masks, flags from the mouth of a dental patient, apples in various stages of mastication. 'No design is a grand design', announces one of the actors, but *The Apple* undermines the epigram, in spite of the many resonances of apples.

When the Living Theatre left the United States, Gelber shifted to less radical subjects and forms – *Square in the Eye* (1965) and *The Cuban Thing* (1968). The protagonist of the former is Ed Stone, New York school teacher and would-be painter, who is scrappily married to Sandy. Beleaguered by Sandy's parents, envious of a painter friend, lusting for that friend's divorced wife, Ed vents his frustrations on his wife. When Sandy dies, Ed abruptly assumes responsibility, cross-examining the crass doctor, and rebelling against Sandy's parents. After a few months, he marries a rich and beautiful woman, but the final scene backtracks to Sandy in the hospital, who closes the play with the vain plea: 'Don't go — Don't Ed.' He may have the painter's eye, but Sandy has been metaphorically struck square in the eye.

The Cuban Thing takes an affluent Cuban family and friends from 1958 to 1964, and a heterogeneous collection they are – free-thinking grandmother, free-living father, avid consumer mother, revolutionary daughter, homosexual son, suave butler, two young intellectuals, as well as a C.I.A. agent. Although Gelber views this play as 'an elaborate pun on sex and politics', which supports the Cuban revolution, it is hard to glean this from the text. Instead, the play shows that the Cuban Revolution has little effect on this middle-class family who continue to live in the same house – less affluent, less secure, but largely untouched by events. Since Gelber directed the play on Broadway – of all places – critic Richard Gilman quipped: 'Gelber's play, which closed after one performance, should never have been allowed by its author to publicly embarrass him the way it did.' On the other hand, misguided pickets should never have been allowed by the producer to close a play, but Broadway responds selectively to pickets. Perhaps that single night on Broadway fosters its author's protective instinct about this play, now his favourite.

Gelber's fifth play *Sleep* (1972) opened Off-Off-Broadway at Wynn Handman's American Place Theatre. Skilfully conceived, it has not received the attention it merits. A divorced young social worker Gil volunteers to be a guinea pig in experiments on sleep. The experimenters are conventionally satirized by their insensitive questions, but the framework permits Gelber to plunge Gil without transition into many situations – professional, racial, erotic, fantastic. At the end of Act I Gil has achieved self-expressive freedom – apparently in a dream, and by Act II he rebels against his questioners, tries to recapture the love of his ex-wife, rejects the facile Karma of the 1960s, and almost dies. Once awake, he leaves the laboratory; the doctors predict that he will return, but it is left an open question. More subtly than in *The Connection*, more coherently than in *The Apple*, Gelber wields a central theatre image; sleep is a play-long metaphor for the way we spend our lives, our very dreams manipulated by impersonal and antisocial forces.

Gelber finds it increasingly difficult to be produced and published, but he maintains his connection with the theatre by teaching and directing. As he approaches the age of fifty, he exemplifies a gifted playwright born in the wrong time or the wrong place: 'It seems to me right now that playwriting is a young man's occupation in America', he said in 1978. After his work with the Living Theatre, he could not imagine fulfilling the demands of Broadway, and yet he could not adapt to Off-Off-Broadway, actually allowing the improvisation whose illusion fascinated him.

Born seven years later (in 1939 in Wakefield, Massachusetts), Israel Horovitz leans in both directions to express the degeneration of modern America. I group him with Actor-Activated playwrights not only because he studied at RADA, then acted and directed himself, but also because his plays were vehicles Off-Off-Broadway for actors who became famous on Broadway or in films – Diane Keaton, Marsha Mason, Al Pacino. In his volume of *Wakefield Plays* Horovitz publishes cast lists for several performances of his plays. He is rumoured to revise readily at actors' suggestions, but his published plays do not bear witness to acting explorations Off-Off-Broadway.

Writing plays from the age of seventeen, Horovitz has had some three dozen plays produced. In 1967 he had four plays Off-Off-Broadway, which he describes amusingly in his collection *First Season*. What he does not mention is the fact that the four plays are written in four styles. In *Rats*, a parable, two gangster-rats fight for a Black baby in Harlem. *It's Called the Sugar Plum* is broad satire with a sentimental end; an accidental death triggers competition between the victim's fellow student and his fiancée, both avid for publicity, and finally taken with one another. *The Indian Wants the Bronx* is a psychological thriller about two young toughs who torture an East Indian trying to locate his son in the Bronx. *Line*, which went on to Broadway, is an Absurdist parable about five people jockeying to be first in line. After that first season, Horovitz couched his parables more realistically, particularly *The Primary English Class* (1975) in which a sexually repressed English teacher interprets the foreign phrases of her students as dark threats.

Horovitz's most extended treatment of American guilt is dramatized in his 'Wakefield Cycle', which was written over a period of seven years, ending 1977. Taking its name from the Massachusetts town in which Horovitz was born (and which puns on the English mystery cycle), his cycle consists of seven plays, as yet unstaged together but intended for five evenings: (1) *Hopscotch* and *The 75th*; (2) *Alfred the Great*; (3) *Our Father's Failing*; (4) *Alfred Dies*; (5) *Stage Directions* and *Spared*.

The opening one-acters gradually reveal acts of betrayal. In *Hopscotch* a 'thirtyish' woman playing hopscotch is greeted by a 'thirtyish' man returning to his home town. By the play's end we learn that he left Wakefield after impregnating the woman when they were both seventeen; intending to settle down with a new wife, he has finished playing sexual hopscotch. The characters are in their nineties in *The 75th* – a high-school reunion. Wasp woman and Jewish man at first fail to recognize one another, but a friendship develops through their recollections of the same childhood friends. The two plays serve (1) to introduce the major theme of betrayal, and (2) to present the characters of the next three plays, which are ambitiously patterned on *The Oresteia*.

Alfred of *Alfred the Great* has made a fortune by selling swamps in the West. He returns to his native Wakefield to seek his brother's murderer. *Our Father's Failing* reveals that Alfred Webber, like Orestes, killed his mother and her lover, but unlike Orestes he has repressed all knowledge of the deed. *Alfred Dies*, like the *Eumenides*, takes the form of a trial. Alfred's Fury-wife Emily charges him with many crimes, and on the Fourth of July she tortures him and condemns him to death. Horovitz strews his trilogy with reminders of Greek tragedy: the family name Webber recalls the pervasive web symbol of Aeschylus; Alfred's wife is his half-sister, recalling the incest in the House of Thyestes; Alfred recognizes Emily's relationship to him through her hair – a scene mocked by Euripides as unrealistic; like Oedipus, Alfred seeks a criminal who proves to be himself.

In asking an audience to accept American incest and murder within a realistic frame, Horovitz takes immense risks. In *Mourning Becomes Electra* O'Neill distanced tragedy to a violent time – the Civil War and its aftermath – and he created in the townspeople an analogue to Greek Chorus, but within a wholly realistic tradition the events are preposterous. Moreover, Horovitz asks us to make immense leaps from the private – Alfred's childhood murder of his mother, adolescent seduction of Margaret, adult marriage to his half-sister – to the public – selling the Indians' land, marrying into a family named Lynch, profiteering on swamps.

The danger of such blatant ambition is mere pretentiousness, which Horovitz seeks to avoid by humour. In *Alfred the Great* Will and Margaret Lynch fling barbs that sting in the manner of Albee's George and Martha. More original are the incomplete jokes of two old fathers in a mental home in *Our Father's Failing*. *Alfred Dies* is grimmer, but the trial barely contains its sadistic thrusts. Since Albee, such thrusts are not infrequent even on Broadway.

Horovitz's last Wakefield evening moves abruptly out of the Webber plot and into experimental forms. *Stage Directions* accurately summarizes the dialogue of that one-acter, in which we witness the reactions to their parents' death of a brother and two sisters. As they keep informing us: 'Richard feels responsible . . . . Ruth feels anger.' Ruby feels grief and may by the play's end be a suicide. A *tour de faiblesse*, the play may also be a parable about the cultural heritage of American Jews. *Spared* is certainly an avatar of the Wandering Jew, eternally 'spared' to tell his tale, which consists of the calamities from which he is spared – in a long monologue heavily imitative of Beckett.

It is possible (but not, I think, probable) that production of the full cycle will create credible continuity for Horovitz's Wakefield plays. With greater verbal dexterity than O'Neill, he lacks that playwright's architectonics and, perhaps more importantly, that playwright's probing morality that is immanent in each work. Working closely with actors Off-Off-Broadway, Horovitz shifted style from realism to filmic violence to beast fable to Absurdism – character studies in frail stories. The Wakefield plays begin in symbolic realism, move on to mythic reach within a realistic straitjacket, and subside into forms so experimental as to read like gimmicks. Always solicitous of his actors, he does not use their discoveries in the plays themselves.

Jean-Claude Van Itallie, born in Belgium in 1936, is the playwright most often associated with the actors' workshops of the Open Theatre. *War and Four Other Plays* (1967) are barely more than sketches; the titular war is a generational conflict between two actors. A role-reversal takes place in *The Hunter and the Bird.* Two skits parody Doris Day of films. *Where is de Queen* is a dream sequence. Beneath the parodic surface ontology may lurk, as suggested by the Doris Day titles *Almost Like Being* and *I'm Really Here.*

What brought Van Itallie to public attention is the *America Hurrah* trilogy, which was not conceived as a trilogy. *Motel* (1962) predates the formation of the Open Theatre. *Interview*, originally entitled *Pavanne* (1965), depends upon their exercises. To round out a full theatre evening Van Itallie quickly wrote *TV* in 1966. The three plays stage aspects of America we are not meant to cheer. They take us on technical adventures: Doll-masks and Voice-over in *Motel,* Choral protagonist in *Interview,* Pirandello for the mass media in *TV.*

Interview stages a Chorus in a series of enactments that function through transformation technique, developed by the Open Theatre. Each actor 'transforms' without transition into a new character-type. The theme – 'Can I help you?' – is answered in an implicit negative since no help comes forth in any of the scenes. The first scene pits Job Applicants against Interviewers, and each successive scene features a single actor-in-type-character frustrated by the Chorus. Actors swiftly transform in situations where they are priest-confessant, psychiatrist-patient, acrobatic opponents, subway riders, square dancers, and, most perniciously, rhetorical politician and silent public. At the last the actors line up 'like marching dolls', one behind the other. They have responded mechanically to their social roles, without hint of sensitivity; that is why no one can help or be helped: 'Can you help me? Next'.

In *TV* George, Hal, and Susan man a television control console, and the play juxtaposes them against the programs they monitor. Van Itallie stipulates: 'The attention of the audience should be focused not on a parody of television, but on the relationship of the life that appears on television to the life that goes on in the viewing room.' In fact, our focus is directed to interacting parodies. Through parallels or contrasts, Van Itallie pairs the halves of his stage: George trying to stop smoking resembles a television monster in lack of self-control over imperious urges; a sexual triangle in the viewing room is paralleled by sexual triangles on television, leading to comparable violence.

When Susan speaks of arranging her apartment, a television couple admires their apartment. At no time do the 'real' characters evince any interest in the news – largely of the Viet War. By the play's end the 'real' characters repeat the exact words of the television characters. On both sides of the screen we see and hear a formulaic, impervious world.

In *Interview* the actors speak in chorus and move 'like marching dolls', but *Motel,* which has often been played alone, is acted by three actors within doll-masks, with heads three times human size. The effect is grotesque – half funny, half fearful. A Man-doll and a Woman-doll are garishly dressed but silent; an incessant Voice-over is associated with a grey Motelkeeper-doll who wears mirror eyeglasses in which audience members glimpse their own reflection. *Motel* is set in an 'anonymously modern' motel and civilization. The Voice-over announces that the room 'will be slashed' as rooms of all civilizations have been destroyed. The voice then utters folksy platitudes about the room we see.

Emerging from behind blinding headlights the Man-doll and the Woman-doll enter the room. The Woman-doll undresses and goes to the offstage bathroom, while the Voice, out of sync with the action, welcomes the guests: 'Modern people like modern places.' The Man-doll undresses, then inspects and strips the bed. From the bathroom come toilet fixtures pell-mell, and the Man-doll begins to dismantle the room. With rock music blaring, with the Voice enumerating a catalogue of incongruous objects – 'cats, catnip, club feet, canisters, banisters, holy books' – the couple draw and write obscenities on the walls; then they twist as though fornicating; soon they tear off the arms of the Motelkeeper-doll. Sirens and rock music drown out the Voice, while the couple behead the Motelkeeper.

Headlights, cacophony, and a rush of air assault the audience. The doll couple walk down the theatre aisle and out of sight, dehumanized and dehumanizing.

Although parody is comfortable on Broadway, Van Itallie's images are still striking – the choral transformations of *Interview*, the echoic clichés of *TV*, and especially the monstrous dolls whose annihilating actions are unsyncopated with a comparably annihilating monologue. *America Hurrah*, an Off-Broadway success, derived in part from actors' exercises of the Open Theatre. *The Serpent: A Ceremony* (1968) won international acclaim for the ensemble. It is easy for a critic to write glibly of playwrights joining Open Theatre improvisations, but the reality entails tensions and disagreements. The personnel of the Open Theatre changed in the years since its founding in 1963, with Joe Chaikin its continuous director, at some personal cost. *America Hurrah* exacerbated strains within the company, some of whom were involved with its success, others with Megan Terry in *Viet Rock*, and still others in workshops of Lee Worley or Rhea Gaisner. With relatively inexperienced actors, Chaikin began a series of improvisational exercises based on *Genesis*, not intended for performance. With professional teachers in different areas – Kristin Linkletter for voice, Peter Kass for acting, Richard Peaslee for singing – the project evolved toward performance almost in spite of the actors, and Chaikin conferred with several writers about scripting the actors' improvisations. Van Itallie finally penned *The Serpent*: 'It wasn't a script that was first written and then performed. It's a script after the fact.'

The Serpent juxtaposes the present against a biblical past in six scenes from *Genesis* – Creation, Temptation of Eve (two scenes), God's curse, the murder of Abel, and Begatting. Van Itallie's narrative traces a paradise lost – for example, God speaks through His creatures, Cain gradually learns to kill, modern women behave like Eve. Into these main scenes Van Itallie inserts smaller acting segments through the Open Theatre technique of 'simultaneous texts', or striking juxtapositions. Thus, we see the Kennedy and King assassinations enacted and re-enacted, along with the reactions of anonymous crowd members: 'I was not involved.' Recollections of individual actors are interwoven into a mime of the ages of man. Finally, the actors sing a sentimental song and walk out through the audience. The ceremony works its way through violence to end in celebration.

As published, *The Serpent* is divided almost equally between scenic description and dialogue, often in free verse lines. New at the first performance was the continual visibility of all fifteen actors, with their informal modern dress, their inventive group images of serpent, Edenic animals, and apple tree. In unusually physical scenes they enact birth, aging, and dying – images that have become clichés *after* the several Open Theatre tours. With the exception of the naïve repetitions of the Temptation scene, Van Itallie's dialogue is spare and dignified, his scenic directions clear and evocative, and the performance is at once a celebration and provocation. In Chaikin's words: 'The text follows the narrative of *Genesis*, and is at the same time a repudiation of its assumptions, thus forming a dialectic.' A dialectic between our cultural heritage and present aculturation.

After intensive work on *The Serpent*, Van Itallie relaxed with short plays and farces. *Mystery Play* (1973) is similar to but not as witty as Tom Stoppard's *Real Inspector Hound*. Both simpler and more ambitious is *A Fable* (1974). A King orders a Journeyor to kill a beast that is devastating his land. The Journeyor justifies her name, travelling to meet

61

various figures with folkloric resonances – a Hermit, two Puppeteers, a Treebeast, a Hanging Person, a Dreamer, A Fugitive, and the Journeyor's 406-year-old Grandmother. Susceptible of several interpretations, each character was developed from actors' exercises. Finally, the dangerous Beast proves to be the King himself, the Journeyor turns into her own grandmother, and the Hanging Person dances jubilantly.

Continuing this penchant for simplicity, Van Itallie produced what is essentially a monodrama, *Bag Lady* (1979). The familiar figure of an urban derelict carries all her belongings with her; her bags are her home. On a November evening in New York City, the bag lady, Clara, feels compelled to discard all but essentials; she therefore has a discard bag and an essentials bag. Her discourse – addressed directly to us, sometimes to passers-by, at deep moments to herself – springs from and returns to the miscellaneous objects in her bag. We learn of her constant hunger through offhand remarks about orange crush, hamburger, peanut butter, egg salad sandwich, baked potato, and brandy. A Russian immigrant who has learned to pretend madness in order to live independently – 'Be a good quiet crazy' – Clara orders her life. Of debilitating thoughts she commands: 'Wipe.' Her fierce intensity rises above the trivial cares of the several passers-by. In a final image Clara sees Nazi brain seeping into the city, which will be snuffed out: 'City's over.' Against that holocaust, she must lighten her load: 'Only essentials.' Although Van Itallie protests in his programme note that 'The play is not an attempt to portray the archetypal bag lady', he may well have accomplished just that. Clara, through illusions of grandeur that are familiar to all of us, through a complex transfer of identity to Mama and doll, through clinging to commodity and yet ordering possessions into bags, through suffering turned to compassion, and through her hard-won freedom, is a very earthy lady. Like Winnie of Beckett's *Happy Days*, she is courageous in the face of catastrophe. Like the Prometheus behind both ladies, she bows to no authority. Disdaining the subway, she emerges from no underworld to assail the heights. In paring her life to essentials, she retains a rare dignity: 'Be a good quiet crazy.'

The Open Theatre brought together playwrights from different parts of the globe. Jean-Claude Van Itallie was born in Belgium, and Megan Terry four years earlier in Seattle. Van Itallie has written for theatre and television whereas Terry was trained in the visual arts. She moved from designing to directing to acting to writing plays. In the mid-1950s in Seattle she staged her own plays (under a pseudonym) along with those of O'Neill, and a reviewer consigned them both to 'a burlesque house on Skid Row' She moved to New York, which was slightly more hospitable. Acting on television, she was

> outraged by the typecasting syndrome and consciously set to work to write plays so it wouldn't matter what type you were as long as you had the talent to play the part. The 'transformation' plays were developed out of this impetus . . . . I wrote *Ex-Miss Copper Queen on a Set of Pills* and *The Magic Realist* and other transformation plays five years before I met Joe Chaikin. When I began to work with the Open Theatre in 1963 it was a conscious decision to recreate theatre as I had dreamed of it, and read of it.

Terry has written over fifty plays, with some two dozen published. Since 1970 she has been associated with the Omaha Magic Theatre.

In spite of what she says, *Ex-Miss Copper Queen* and *The Magic Realist* are not transformation plays, but eight of her plays were produced by the Open Theatre. Stemming from child's play and actor's improvisations, transformation plays broaden the actor's technical skill, since he or she has to shift sex, age, class, or even enact a lifeless object. Terry's first transformation *Eat at Joe's* is unpublished, but the technique is graphically illustrated in *Keep Tightly Closed in a Cool Dry Place* (1965). The title derives from instructions on foodstuff containers, but Terry implicitly commands the actor, too, to keep emotions cool while enacting the immediate situation, as in Diderot's *Paradox of the Actor*. In *Keep Tightly Closed* three men are in the same jail for murdering the wife of one of them. Without warning, they transform into General Custer's soldiers dismembering an Indian, into Captain John Smith saving two members of his expedition. Other transformations incorporate and revolve about the scene of the murder. In amassing the circumstantial evidence, Terry ingeniously portrays media caricatures – entertainers, drag queens, movie gangsters, altar boys, as well as machines. It is problematical whether, as the first directors claim, these transformations add to 'a visceral understanding of guilt', but they do provide scope for the actor to parody aspects of popular culture.

Terry has described *Comings and Goings* (1966) as 'a trampoline for actors and director'. The number of actors varies, but the individual human scenes are built around he – she exchanges; the actors also portray electric plugs, a pencil and list, signalling galaxies, and they close on a celebratory courtship scene. That same year Terry wrote her favourite play *The Gloaming, Oh My Darling*, which is not a transformation. Two old women in a rest home share a man, or perhaps a fantasy of a man, Mr Birdsong.

Temperamentally mercurial, the two bedridden women shift mood as swiftly as Terry's other characters shift roles, and Mr Birdsong intones at intervals a jingoistic view of American history. Inspired by him, Mrs Tweed and Mrs Watermellon revert to their youth, resist their nurse, and finally move into the gloaming of death.

Terry's major work with Open Theatre actors is *Viet Rock* (1966), subtitled a 'Folk War Movie'. It is a movie in its transformational 'cut' after each scene, and in the popular culture characters at the base of the scenes. The actors assume a dozen different roles during the course of an action that traces American involvement in Vietnam, from induction into the Army through unspeakable cruelties on both sides to the final circle of corpses, 'the reverse of the beautiful circle of the opening image'. Built on group improvisation, free in its transformations, the play does not accomplish Terry's stated objective of 'getting at the essence of violence', but it does present strong group images.

Even before the Open Theatre disbanded in 1973, Megan Terry brought their improvisation techniques to other theatres, professional and amateur. In co-operation with students at the innovative Immaculate Heart College of Los Angeles, she developed her *Tommy Allen Show*. A parody of a television talk show, the play is predicated on the fragmentary character of that form. The audience moves through fifteen areas before being seated in a television studio to be subjected to the all-American clichés of Tommy Allen (analogous to Terrence McNally's Tommy Flowers). In an abrupt change of scene, the sixteen actors undergo various physical tortures, each repeating an anguished monologue whenever the audience approaches.

Approaching Simone was written for the Boston University centennial in 1970, but it also marks a break with

Terry's parodies of the 1960s, since Simone Weil is a wholly sympathetic protagonist, about whom Terry said in an interview: 'I have been consciously building my technique so that I could write a play about her.' The role of Simone Weil combines two types – philosopher and saint – who are notoriously difficult to stage.

Terry's staging is quite elaborate as she traces Weil's life from childhood to willed martyrdom. As a child, Simone carries heavy burdens, spurns stockings lacking to the poor, and refuses sugar lacking to soldiers. At fourteen she is tempted by suicide but rises above it: 'Focus on the dark inside your head.' As an adult she dances with a Black American singer. She is twice discharged from teaching positions for dedication beyond the classroom, and she turns happily to factory work.

Act I might be called the Abjuration of self, with Act II the Immersion in Community – a union activist in her factory, a volunteer in the Spanish Civil War, a Christian inspired by the poems of George Herbert, a Jewish refugee in Marseille, a participant in Harlem gospel services, and finally a London volunteer for the Free French during the Second World War. Assigned to clerical work rather than the dangerous mission she requests, Simone starves herself to death, refusing food as she once refused sugar unavailable to her compatriots.

Terry's modesty is evident in her title *Approaching Simone*, but her saint is less dramatic than Corneille's Polyeucte or Eliot's Thomas, for Simone faces small opposition to her dedication. Terry's scenic images are inventive – elaborate planes against which the action unfolds, Simone's self-doubt physicalized by white poultices of increasing size, her shoving bourgeois furniture into the orchestra pit, the activities of Simone's students who recite and hike through the audience, human machines in

66

the factory, revolving pyramids as Simone lectures, Chorus members donning Simone's garments as they fall, the increasingly tall and fat figures of the Free French in London, the Chorus become a pile of war corpses, and, finally, Simone's climb to the highest ramp for her sainthood.

After this ambitious drama of homage, Terry relaxed with slighter works – several committed to feminism. Her next extended drama, *Hothouse* (1974), is thought to show that 'strength is passed down from one woman to another', but the play actually rollicks through three generations of hard-drinking, hard-loving women joined in a thin plot and marred by what is unusual in Terry's full-length plays – obedience to old conventions of family realism. Back at her home base of Omaha Magic Theatre Terry presented that theatre's most popular piece, *Babes in the Bighouse, a Documentary Musical Fantasy about Life in a Women's Prison* (1974). Blending documentary research, the cell effects of the Living Theatre *Frankenstein*, and Open Theatre transformations, Terry examines a special feminist area – prison. With neither the relentless brutality of *The Brig* nor the simulated torture of realistic stage jails, *Babes in the Bighouse* stages the abyss between behaviour and punishment, desire and fulfilment, loneliness and enforced company. Without linear plot, the three men and three women ('babes' are played by both sexes) transform in several roles based on improvisations, but they nevertheless trace continuous prison life.

Co-operating willingly with prisoners, students, or feminists, Terry worked with the last group on dramatizing the sexism of our language. *American Kings English for Queens* (1978) is a witty but confusing title, since 'queens' in today's slang means male homosexuals and not women, much less feminists. Through scenes centred on the family, that bourgeois cell that was anathema in the 1960s, the masculinity of the English language is depicted. Adopting the feral child Morgan, the family's oldest daughter realizes: 'We'll have to think of a way we can teach her to talk without making her feel that being a girl is not as good as being a boy.' With the help of a cranky, music, and ebullient animal drives, the family succeed theatrically, if not humanistically, since the play ends in song: 'When is a human being, Being a human being?'

Although *Attempted Rescue on Avenue B* (1979) is subtitled 'A Beat Fifties Comic Opera', it is actually a realistic play set in New York City's East Village between 1958 and 1960. At the beginning of three acts, aspiring actress Mira Anderson moves into the small Avenue B apartment of painter Landy Taverniti. The play traces their craggy relationship, as well as the demands of their respective arts. By the end of the play Landy's father has committed suicide, their best friend Maxine has died of cancer, another friend has deserted art for politics. Terry evokes Bohemia in the 1950s, down to the abstract expressionist process of painting, and the Method explorations of acting. In a larger context *Rescue* is Terry's attempt to rescue the avant-garde of the 1950s from contempt by the 1970s.

Versatile, energetic, endlessly inventive, Megan Terry has created many many plays that have provided pleasure and/or instruction to different co-workers and many kinds of audiences. Often vivid in immediacy, her plays rarely attain the fusion of phrase to image, which distinguishes durable drama.

Less prolific, Maria Irene Fornès also endows the Off-Off-Broadway scene with several talents. Of Cuban birth (in 1930), she is doubly trilingual; her formal languages are Spanish, English, French, and her artistic languages are designing, directing, playwriting. Her single volume of published plays shows meticulous attention to visual as well as verbal detail. Slight on the surface, they are surprisingly memorable. Floating away from realism, they offer an oblique critique of reality.

Her first play announces the incisive thrust of her light touch. Although developed traditionally for the Actor's Workshop of San Francisco, *Tango Palace* (1961) displays her concern with acting rather than plot or character development. The tango palace designates the habitat and shrine of Isidore, 'an androgynous clown', into which is born an earnest youth Leopold, crawling out of a sack in a business suit. Leopold is a rationalist, seeking logic and sequence, but inventive Isidore moves by caprice, and among his movements is the titular tango. The action of *Tango Palace* pivots on the duel of Isidore and Leopold, with the former highly conscious of the articulation of that duel. 'Each time Isidore feels he has said something important, he takes a card from his pocket or from a drawer and flips it across the room in any direction.' By the end of the play their battle-ground, the tango palace, is strewn with cards. When Leopold threatens to burn them, Isidore warns him that he will die. When Leopold actually sets fire to a card, Isidore trips him and exclaims: 'There! You died.' – the play's first title. But Leopold does not die. He pleads for cessation of cards, for egress from the room. Isidore regales him (and us) with a parable of a rat slain by the man who loved him, of a beetle with dirt inside him. Leopold counters with a tale of a crawling snake, as he himself crawls. Leopold refuses to continue their duel. He plunges a sword into Isidore, who promptly appears as an angel, still carrying cards. The play ends when 'Leopold walks through the door slowly, but with determination. He is ready for the next stage of their battle.'

Fornès' next play, *The Successful Life of 3* (1965), was created with the Open Theatre, thriving on humour and spurning psychology in an extended pun on an eternal triangle. He and She are a couple, and a rival, 3, vies for She's love. The play traces their intertwined lives from first meeting in a doctor's office where She is a nurse, through the marriage of He and She, the desertion of He by She, She's return to a household of He and 3, He as detective arresting 3 as thief, 3's adventures with police and body-guards, and a final joyous reunion of the three. As compared to Noel Coward's *Design for Living*, Fornès' play is an *Un*design for living a successful life of three – successful because of its inventiveness. Like Bergman's *Scenes from a Marriage*, these scenes from a triangle, arbitrary as to time and place, are emblematic of sexual affinities in our culture.

Promenade was written soon after *The Successful Life of 3*, and even the revised published version shows its proximity. This time the play presents the zany adventures of two triangles – the prisoners 105 and 106 and their mother, on the one hand, and the same men with a female companion, on the other. Digging their way out of prison, the two men attend a banquet, where they steal everything portable, including a woman whom they drape in their loot. Suddenly, they are joined by their mother to comfort soldiers on a battlefield. Then they are imprisoned again, along with mother and woman. Finally alone in jail, they sing: 'All is well in the city . . . . And for those who have no cake,/There's plenty of bread.'

With *Dr Kheal* (1968) Fornès' satire becomes more overt. Like Dr Kheal's predecessors, Ionesco's teacher in *The Lesson* and Adamov's Professor Taranne, Fornès' professor takes a stance of omniscience, which is shaken in the play's action. Unlike his forerunners, however, Dr

Kheal unbalances his *own* omniscience, with the self-contradiction implicit in his name that contains 'heal' and 'kill': '/Reality/ is opposites, contradictions compressed so that you don't know where one stops and the other begins.' As Fornès' Isidore consigned his wisdom to cards, Dr Kheal consigns his wisdom to the blackboard, where he expounds on Poetry, Balance, Ambition, Energy, Speech, Truth, Beauty, Love, Hope, and anticlimactically, Cooking. Illustrating with figures and drawings, he arrives at ignorance rather than knowledge: 'Man is the rational animal.' And that is his undoing.

In *Molly's Dream* (1968) Fornès for the first time presents a rational structure for her surreal associations. The action is set in an old-fashioned saloon where waitress Molly looks at a Young Man. She leans her head on a table, falls asleep, and dreams most of the rest of the play, which gradually narrows down to herself and the young man as Jim. Actually, he leaves the saloon before she awakens. She opens her eyes and gazes at the spot where he sat – now empty of the several whimsical characters of popular culture. Less successful are characters of popular culture in an anti-war play *The Red Burning Light of Mission XQ 3* (1969).

During the 1970s Fornès' administrative work for Theatre Strategy left her reduced time for playwriting. Of three plays of these years – *The Curse of the Langston House* (1972), *Aurora* (1973), and *Fefu and her Friends* (1977), only the last has been published. In it the audience moves with the actresses through the rooms of a New England country house: living room to lawn to study to bedroom to kitchen and back to living room, there to watch scenes between Fefu, nickname for Stephany Beckman, and her seven women friends. Unlike Fornès' earlier plays activated by actors, this subtly feminist drama appears to be activated by shifting environments.

Although Fornès has called the play plotless, a nuanced plot is traceable through the several groupings of these eight women who meet in Fefu's house on a spring day in 1935. Aside from hostess Fefu (married to Phillip, who never appears), there is Julia in her wheelchair, the pair Christina and Cindy, histrionic Emma, ex-lovers Paula and Cecilia, and Sue who is least individualized. Fefu has been toying with a gun before her guests arrive. The purpose of the women's meeting is to raise funds for supporting art as a tool of learning, with actual quotations from 'The Science of Educational Dramatics' by Emma Sheridan Fry. After the fund drive rehearsal, a few women go to the kitchen ostensibly to make coffee, but they actually engage in a water-fight. Fefu is quite suddenly brutal to Julia, insisting that she can walk, that she can combat the deadly forces that she hallucinates. Interrupted by Christina, Fefu takes her gun outside. A shot is soon heard, and Julia bleeds from her forehead. Fefu re-enters with a dead rabbit, stands behind bleeding Julia, and utters the play's closing line: 'I killed it . . . I just shot . . . and killed it . . . Julia.' The others surround Julia as the light fades.

Wounded though she is, Julia triumphs over Fefu whose hesitancies cast doubt on her ability to kill 'it'. Although the innovative staging calls for the audience participation that was a tenet of the 1960s, the play is true to Fornès' own major theme – the triumph of the irrational. Through another environment, Fefu and Julia continue the duel of Leopold and Isidore of *Tango Palace* into 'the next stage of their battle'.

This chapter was devoted to a few playwrights who began Off-Off-Broadway, who worked closely with actors. Although Jack Gelber now reads like a traditionalist, he joined the Living Theatre at the time the Becks were formulating the radical aesthetic that influenced theatres throughout the world. (I will glance in the next chapter at their collective plays.) The Living Theatre's most methodical non-Method actor, Joe Chaikin, founded the Open Theatre with the actor at its aesthetic centre, but the group welcomed the assistance of other theatre artists, including playwrights. Jean-Claude Van Itallie, Megan Terry, Irene Fornès produced a body of plays seeded by actors' exercises, particularly transformation. At the same time, in neighbouring unconventional spaces, other actors deliberately cultivated a rough style or emotional crescendos, which are reflected in plays of Israel Horovitz. The Open Theatre was almost alone in *disciplining* the heterogeneous energies of Off-Off-Broadway in the 1960s. In that heady time, the new young Left cried out and sometimes fought for all kinds of freedom – artistic, sexual, political, social – and the Off-Off-Broadway theatre amplified those cries. By 1970, however, Jean-Claude Van Itallie declared:

> Perhaps five years or so after it was born, the Off-Off-Broadway movement has become moribund; dying perhaps of too much attention, and also because the action has moved away from the theater . . . . Where is the vital current? In America it's in the political movements, the rock concerts and the communes.

But even the most participatory theatre could never match the 'vital current' of political movements, rock concerts, or communes. Rather than dying from too much attention, Off-Off-Broadway inevitably fell prey to attack by time. As young theatre amateurs grew older, they moved in the 1970s either toward professionalism or, more often, away from theatre. A very small percentage persisted in their craft, which involved its own transformations.

73

5
Agit, Prop, and Radical Idiom: the Becks, Holden, Valdez

1968 is the Year of the Radical. A new KKK threatened the land in the Killing of King and Kennedy. One of the year's less violent events was the birth of the Radical Theatre Repertory, which proclaimed:

> The member groups, and dozens of others in this country and abroad, are in the vanguard of a new phenomenon in theatrical and social history – the spontaneous generation of communal playing troupes, sharing voluntary poverty, making experimental collective creations and exploring space, time, minds, and bodies in manifold new ways to meet the demands of our explosive period.

With the exception of the Firehouse Theatre in Minneapolis (but soon thereafter in San Francisco), the nineteen radical groups of the Repertory were located on the two coasts of the United States, thirteen in New York. Although the members probably agreed on opposition to the war in Vietnam, over half of them were not overtly political. A decade afterwards, six of the nineteen groups

were still playing, and only three were politically radical –
the Living Theatre, the San Francisco Mime Troupe, and
El Teatro Campesino.

The 'new phenomenon' was not quite new, for 'commun-
al playing troupes' date back half a century to the Russian
Revolution. The phrase 'agit-prop' entered the English
language by way of Russian; the O.E.D. records its earliest
use in 1934, as a translation of the Russian *agitatsiya-
propaganda*: 'A department of the Central Committee of
the Russian Communist Party responsible . . . for "agitation and propaganda" on behalf of Communism.' An easily
naturalized phrase, agit-prop early sought theatre outlets.
In the 1930s – what the late lamented Harold Clurman
called 'the fervent years' – American agit-prop theatre
sprang up in unions, neighbourhoods, and the federally
financed Works Project Administration; sprang up and
often collapsed with the moment's crisis. Nevertheless,
such theatre led to the formation of the Actor's Studio and
the Method-acting empire, which later penetrated all
countries through Hollywood films. Few contemporary
American actors are unmarked by acting styles of the
fervent years; in that period drama also broadened its
subject matter and occasionally its idiom. Playwrights
Robert Ardrey, Paul Green, Lillian Hellman, Clifford
Odets, Elmer Rice, William Saroyan, Irwin Shaw were
nurtured by the radical theatre of the 1930s, mainly within
traditional theatre format: the playwright delivers a script,
which the director casts not only with actors but also with
designers and technicians. To each his own speciality; with
luck and skill, performances might cohere.

The radicals of the 1960s often rejected specialities,
including that of the writer. The Radical Repertory credo
of 1968 speaks of 'exploring space, time, minds, and
bodies', but not language. And yet political radicals were

less suspicious of words than performance radicals in the wake of Artaud. Politically radical theatres deploy words in two main ways – either as weapons hurled at the audience or as barbs stinging them to laughter. One *or* the other tends to dominate any given radical play.

The Living Theatre achieved international – as opposed to New York City – celebrity through its assault arsenal. As this book goes to press – 1981 – a middle-aged American couple live on the outskirts of Rome. Ardent pacifists, Julian Beck and Judith Malina have shared an embattled life. Their story, a modern saints' legend, has been told several times in several tongues. Meeting in 1943 while still in their teens, founding a theatre in 1947, they staged non-commercial plays by W. H. Auden, Bert Brecht, Jean Cocteau, Paul Goodman, Garcia Lorca, Gertrude Stein, W. C. Williams. Their *succès de scandale*, as discussed in the last chapter, is associated with two playwrights whom they produced in the early 1960s – Jack Gelber's junkie *Connection* and Kenneth Brown's Marine *Brig*. Revolting against theatre conventions for these radical scripts, the Becks infused their Living Theatre with a new vision – living as theatre and theatre as living. Never was a theatre more presciently named. For more than three decades Beck and Malina have been tireless leaders, speakers, performers. They have been arrested, beaten, adored, subsidized. The Becks have written books, Judith a journal for 1968–9 (*The Enormous Despair*) and Julian a meditation on theatre between 1962–72 (*The Life of the Theatre*). Judith Malina and Julian Beck became familiar names to people who had never seen them in the flesh. They were photographed dirty, naked, maniacal, and yet they retain their dignity. No one calls them Judie and Julie.

Optimistically, Beck hoped: 'The theater is the Wooden Horse by which we can take the town.' It is easy today to sneer that no town has been taken by these combative anarchists. But the Becks have taken the imagination of a young generation in the 1960s; their Wooden Horse is personal example, including the example of public performance. Their martyrdom begins in 1963, when their New York City theatre was padlocked for non-payment of taxes, although they charged that the true cause was performance of the anti-militarist *Brig*. Released on bail to fulfil a European engagement, the Becks returned to jail in their own country. For five years after that, they and their company wandered around Europe, collaborating on creations in thirteen different countries. Although few of these creations originated in words, the scripts were later published, and it is by virtue of such publication that the theatrical Becks may be classified as dramatists.

Mysteries and Smaller Pieces (1964) consists of a dozen scenes, and words are uttered – sparingly – in only three; they figure importantly in only one – 'Street Songs'. The scenic directions indicate the new performance strategy of the Living Theatre: 'No curtain./ Performers circulate among audience. Everyday clothes./ Performers become part of audience./Contacts.' Contacts rarely meant words. The first silent scene recapitulates *The Brig*, with its inhuman imposition of mechanical motions. In the second scene, 'The Dollar Poem', the words on a dollar are recited chorally to strict choreography. An Indian *Raga* is followed by wordless processions of performers among spectators. In 'Street Songs' two-beat agitational slogans are chanted by a single actor in random order, and these words are echoed by performers seated among the spectators. When these actors move to the stage, still chanting, they invite the audience to join them in a large circle. Everyone hums, breathes, exercises rhythmically.

After an intermission, the actors perform intricate

tableaux vivants with rectangular white boxes. Then they perform transformational exercises, passing sound and gesture from individual to individual. These 'smaller pieces' prepare the final scene of an Artaudian plague, a mystery. Each Living Theatre performer enacts a death by plague. In Leslie Epstein's description: 'A body shudders, a mouth opens, closes, a rattle, a sigh, silence around me now, people fall from their seats, kneel by the dying, embrace them.' When the company lies rigid and scattered, 'survivors' carry the 'corpses' centre stage, remove their shoes, stroke contorted limbs, and pile them neatly one on top of another, five on the bottom layer, then four, three, two, and one. At the last we behold a grotesquely harmonious pyramid, silent but crying out to and against passive spectators.

The next two productions of the Living Theatre retreat to fiction – *Frankenstein* (1965) and *Antigone* (1966) which alone credits the writer of the text: 'Translated into English by Judith Malina, from Hölderlin's German and Brecht's adaptation.' After these performances, the company felt imprisoned by scripts. *Paradise Now* (1968) was therefore a deliberate return to the verbal paucity and ritual gestures of *Mysteries*, but it was also a deliberate step away from the evil depicted in fiction. In Beck's words: 'We wanted to make a play which would no longer be an enactment but would be the act itself.'

Paradise Now, like *Mysteries* four years earlier, grew from company improvisation. Unlike the fairly discrete scenes of *Mysteries*, however, *Paradise Now* is meant to be a continuous journey, which is also a 'trip'. There are eight stages or processes to the journey, each with its own Rite, Vision, and Action. (These are the published titles, but it was hard in performance to differentiate Rite from Vision or mere image.) A blend of dark night of the soul, Kabbala,

I Ching, Tantric Buddhism, the performance lasts four to five hours, always losing spectators before the end. Rites and Visions were performed for spectators, but Actions were an open invitation for audience participation.

The Living Theatre programme lists eight rungs of the climb to Paradise. Rung IV, entitled 'Universal Intercourse', was sensational in 1968; certain spectators enthusiastically entered an orgy while others departed in disgust. By Rung VIII the participants of the new Paradise moved out into the open air. In spite of the title – *'Paradise Now'* – the performance was most forceful in infernoes, when the theatre crowd was harrassed by repressive agents but shouted defiantly: 'Free theatre. The theatre is yours. Act. Speak. Do whatever you want.'

Having asserted freedom in *Paradise Now*, the Living Theatre turned its collective back on formal theatres. In Beck's words: 'Abandon the theatres. Create other circumstances for the man in the street. Create circumstances that will lead to Action, which is the highest form of theatre we know.' In 1970 the collective divided into four groups in four countries. The Beck portion went to Sao Paulo, Brazil, where they conceived an ambitious project, *The Legacy of Cain*, a performance cycle that was envisioned to grow to 150 pieces. Deported from Brazil to the United States, the Beck Living Theatre at first engaged in agit-prop on current issues, especially the Viet War, but by 1973 they developed the first extended spectacle of *The Legacy*, *Seven Meditations on Political SadoMasochism*. Malina wrote the first meditation, and the group chose other texts to form the basis of the remaining six. In contrast to the confrontation tactics of the 1960s, the actors encircled the audience in a collective embrace.

At the company headquarters in Brooklyn toward the end of 1973, they began work on *The Money Tower*, another Cain piece that was, ironically, funded by the Mellon Foundation. Physical structure and scenario displayed the hierarchy of the *Cain* society – our own. As in 'Street Songs' of *Mysteries*, the words are chanted: 'This is the House that money built.' Occasionally, sentences recall the hopeful 1930s: 'The workers will organize the work and there will be no more money and no more money system and we will all be free.' Moving to Pittsburgh in 1974, the Living Theatre performed another piece of the *Cain* cycle, *Six Public Acts to Transmute Violence into Concord*. The title indicates how far they had travelled from the furious 1960s, but they remembered the theatre of those years, recycling phrases from *Mysteries* and shapes from *Frankenstein*. Not that their powers of invention were flagging, but they wanted to demonstrate the consistency of their political anarchy and biomechanical aesthetics.

In 1975 the Becks started on what they anticipated as a European tour, but it turned out to be extended exile in Rome, where they live from performance to performance, more or mostly less subsidized, sporadically adding pieces to the *Cain* cycle, and most recently preoccupied with a reworking of *Prometheus* (1979). The rebel god becomes the American anarchist Alexander Berkman, and Io becomes Emma Goldman, very different from that of Rochelle Owens. The whole looks back on their 1950s taste for plays within plays, since the director of this *Prometheus* is Lenin, played by Beck. Faithful to the participatory aesthetics of the 1960s, the performance forces an audience to choose sides in the storming of the Russian Winter Palace. News reports of this production do not indicate whether words are spoken.

In its unique history, the Living Theatre has encouraged few living playwrights. After *Paradise Now*, however, the Becks have freely offered their nominally collective scripts:

'The play "Paradise Now" is not private property:/ there are no performance royalties to pay:/ it is free:/ for any community that wants to play it.' Other communities have occasionally performed Living Theatre scripts of the last decade, but their impact is considerably diminished.

Two other long-term radical theatres offer scripts that have been performed widely. In 1968 a radical theatre festival was held at San Francisco State University, involving three groups – Peter Schuman's Bread and Puppet Theatre, Ronnie Davis's San Francisco Mime Troupe, and Luis Valdez's Teatro Campesino each dominated by the strong personality of its founding father. Unlike New York's Living Theatre, the San Francisco Mime Troupe and El Teatro Campesino played in California's mild climate. The Living Theatre agitated its audience, stirring up guilt in the 1960s, requesting complicity in the 1970s. The San Francisco Mime Troupe and El Teatro Campesino have a less radical aesthetic and a more radical message, inclining toward propaganda rather than agitation. Moreover, their propaganda beguiles audiences with no experience of theatre, since their main genre is broad comedy.

The San Francisco Mime Troupe was founded in 1959 by Ronnie Davis, who had trained as a mime. During the 1960s the loosely organized but very vocal troupe hesitated between enacting political sketches or staging aesthetic events. By 1967 the group had evolved a modified *commedia* style for park performance, and radical politics triumphed over radical aesthetics. Performances were short, pungent, and penned by any writer corralled by Davis. In 1970 a cohesive theatre group declared itself a collective whose main purpose was to perform political plays in Bay Area parks. Davis resigned.

This collective was in no sense an imitation of the Living

Theatre. The members did not live communally, and they did not claim universal theatre skills. Rather, they were a political and economic collective, each member drawing the same salary but exercising his or her main skill. Most of the members were performers, but a non-performer, Joan Holden, gradually evolved as the company's main dramatist; she is given at least partial credit for six of the eight plays published in the troupe anthology *By Popular Demand*.

Popular demand greeted Holden's first play for the collective Mime Troupe. Unlike her adaptations under the aegis of Ronnie Davis, *The Independent Female* (1970) was patterned on melodrama rather than *commedia*. Both forms manipulate the old formula of Greek New Comedy – a pair of lovers overcoming an obstacle to their union. In *commedia* the obstacle is a stock comic – Pantalone, Il Dottore, Il Capitano. In the Mime Troupe's modified *commedia* these masked acrobatic figures are satirized representatives of capitalism, but in Holden's modified melodrama the obstacle is a young woman's nascent independence. When the heroine's friend, a veteran feminist, is killed – 'My epitaph: "Shot in her back for refusing to live on it." ' – the *ingénue* resolutely rejects her sexist lover. Holden's happy ending is not the traditional coupling, but a determined sisterhood of independent females.

As Holden's *Independent Female* (1970) subverts soap opera, her *Dragon Lady's Revenge* (1971) subverts the comic strip (*Terry and the Pirates*). Provoked by C.I.A. involvement in Vietnam drug traffic, *The Dragon Lady's Revenge* is intricately plotted by four members of the Mime Troupe, but the dialogue is largely Holden's. In the 'fictional' land of Long Penh, the American Ambassador explains the presence of his country's armed forces: 'Basically, we are here because we desperately want to get out.' While 'here', his Lieutenant son becomes a junkie at the Dragon Lady's bar, one of the enterprises of a mysterious Mr Big. A barmaid Blossom tries vainly to detoxify him. A C.I.A. agent Drooley hisses through his several disguises of priest, fakir, Jesus freak, fencer, and nun. When the Dragon Lady wants to kill General Rong Q over drug profits, the latter reveals that the American Ambassador is an old lover who abandoned her, as in Von Sternberg's *Lady from Shanghai*. All members of the cast slink into the Dragon Lady's bar, murder in their hearts and assorted weapons. Agent Drooley drinks a poisoned cocktail, and General Rong Q is stabbed in the back with a giant syringe. Mr Big is literally unmasked as the American Ambassador, whom the Dragon Lady attacks with another syringe. When the Ambassador turns that theatrical weapon against her, Blossom covers him with a machine gun. She will exhibit the criminal Mr Big through the villages of Long Penh, denouncing his crimes.

AMBASSADOR: They'll never believe it; they're too stupid.
BLOSSOM: They get smarter every day.

The promise of a smart people's victory is the unsuspecting Dragon Lady's revenge.

Holden's next play shifted from global to local politics, revising *High Rises*, a collective Mime Troupe script based on a story of one of its members. In San Francisco, real-estate interests succeeded in demolishing the International Hotel that housed elderly tenants. (Seven years later, the hotel's ghost hovers over a huge hole.) With fellow-trouper Steve Friedman, Holden grounded *San Fran Scandals of 1973* on a popular American genre, musical comedy. Frank and Stella, an old couple who were once the musical comedy team of Burns and Barnes, are about to be evicted so that their home can be torn down to make room for a cultural centre. The villain is a Mr Smellybucks, who does not appreciate his singing secretary but idolizes opera stars like Carlotta Snotta. Mistaking Stella for Carlotta, Smellybucks inadvertently gives a contract to the old vaudevillian, and she then persuades him to spare the old building. In a musical dénouement, Smellybucks' singing secretary proves to be the long-lost daughter of Burns and Barnes.

Frijoles (1975) fans out to a global subject – food. *Frijoles* is Spanish for beans, and this is the nourishing crop of a couple in an unnamed South American country, until a United States company imposes cultivation of exportable bananas. Miserable under Yankee exploitation, the Latino couple enclose a note in a banana shipment, which is discovered by an American couple who are struggling against inflation: 'It took me three hours to get through the express lane at the supermarket – nobody can afford more than six items.' High on the political totem pole, Butz and Kissinger attend an international food conference in Rome: 'To eat, or not to eat – that is the question. Or more precisely, who is to eat, and who is not to eat.' Both oppressed couples arrive in Rome, the Latinos stowing away in a banana cargo and the Americans winning a free flight. Hungry, both couples steal food and then denounce the conference. Realizing that they are class as well as pen pals, they gladly feast on beans.

By 1976, the year of America's Bicentennial, Holden was thoroughly at home in her chosen idiom, geared to a small stage and the open air. Her swift scenes in simple diction accumulated into a clean story line. In contrast to more experimental playwrights, she thrives on linear, spirited narration that displays characters with clear responses to the class struggle.

The Becks, Holden, Valdez

For the Bicentennial the San Francisco Mime Troupe wanted a play about underground American history – the unsung stories of labour, women, minorities. The seventeen troupe members read avidly, but they managed to choose a subject only when their European tour loomed close. Almost by default, Holden produced the company's longest and most ambitious script, *False Promises/Nos Engañaron*. Set during the Spanish-American War, the play is fictionalized history of a Colorado mine strike. Not only is the plot intricate, but also it shifts locale from Washington to Puerto Rico to various parts of Copper City, Colorado. Upper-echelon figures like J. P. Morgan, Teddy Roosevelt, President McKinley, and their minions are candid caricatures; as in Brecht plays, they speak blank verse or heroic couplets: 'Thy holy mission we accept, Oh Lord./ We'll teach democracy with fire and sword.' New to Holden's dramaturgy is the heightened realism of the working-class characters, in their strength and weakness.

Like Holden's earlier plays, *False Promises* pits rapacious capitalists against exploited workers, but within her working-class milieu there is telling contrast between a naïve Black soldier Washington Jefferson, a naïve patriotic miner Harry Potter, a socialist miner Casey, a Mexican miner's widow Maria, a Black saloon-owner Montana, a corrupt union-leader Charlie Slade. Prevented from voting in his native South Carolina, Washington Jefferson is persuaded by Teddy Roosevelt to join 'a coloured regiment' of the United States Army, where he fights in Puerto Rico and learns first hand about American imperialism. He is then sent to Copper City, Colorado, to quell a miners' strike. Mine-owners have exploited workers and encouraged strife between Mexicans and Anglos. When the miners unite to strike, wives and saloon singers support them, turning back a trainload of scabs. As the strike continues, however, with its privations, the miners' unity collapses. It is at this point that Washington Jefferson arrives with orders to arrest the strikers. He reports that the socialist Casey has been hanged.

Holden, wishing to be hopeful without preaching, tried three different endings : (1) Washington Jefferson triumphantly reunifies the strikers; (2) Washington is shot, and Harry Potter takes up the struggle; (3) Montana convinces Washington not to arrest the strikers, and the fate of all is left open. The first version is published in *By Popular Demand*, with Washington teaching: 'When the time come, you don't get to pick who's on your side – history decide that for you. You just got to understand history.'

Later, as yet unpublished Holden plays continue this realistic depiction of confusion in the working class – *Squash* on the energy crisis, *Electrobucks* on the computer industry, *Factperson* on media misinformation and trivialization. Like Brecht, Holden views her plays as *Versuche*, experiments subject to change in performance – not only in rehearsal but also in actual performance, which she attends assiduously. The antithesis of a lonely writer dependent on inspiration, she visualizes particular Mime Troupe actors speaking her lines, even though the lines may actually fall to others. When Holden talks about her plays, she says *scripting* rather than writing; plays may form in several heads, but her own two hands pound out the words of a playable draft – playable by other troupes as well as the Mime Troupe.

Luis Valdez is the most Protean of today's radical dramatists. Actor and director as well as playwright, he founded El Teatro Campesino in 1965, which became the heart of *El Centro Campesino Culturál*. Born into a large family of migrant farmworkers in 1940, Valdez did not learn English until he attended school in California. As a

1. Playwright Neil Simon

2. *Duck Variations* by David Mamet. Photo: Ron Blanchette

3. *Alfred Dies* by Israel Horowitz. Photo: Ron Blanchette

4. *The Connection* by Jack Gelber. Photo: © Alix Jeffry 1981/Harvard Theatre Collection

5. *Motel* by Jean-Claude van Itallie. Photo: Niblock/Bough

6. *Bag Lady* by Jean-Claude van Itallie. Photo: Nathaniel Tileston

7. Playwright Amiri Baraka (LeRoi Jones)

8. *Dutchman* by LeRoi Jones. Photo: © Alix Jeffry 1981/Harvard Theatre Collection

9. *The Corner* by Ed Bullins. Photo: Friedman-Abeles

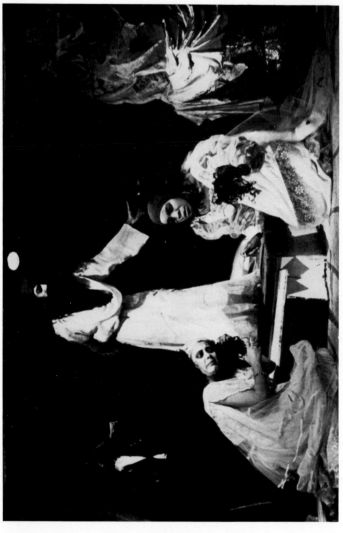

10. *Funnyhouse of a Negro* by Adrienne Kennedy. Photo: © Alix Jeffry, 1961/Harvard Theatre Collection

11. *Bluebeard by* Charles Ludlam. Photo: Thomas Harding

12. *The Moke-Eater* by Kenneth Bernard. Photo: Robert A. Propper

13. *Night Club* by Kenneth Bernard. Photo: Allan Tepper

14 *Minnie Mouse and the Tap-Dancing Buddha* by Michael McClure. Photo: Ron Blanchette

15. *Pandering to the Masses: A Misrepresentation* by Richard Foreman. Photo: Theodore Shank

16. *The Red Horse Animation* by Lee Breuer. Photo: Theodore Shank

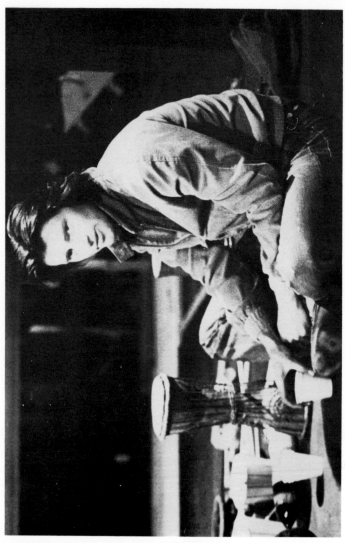
17. Playwright Sam Shepard. Photo: Ron Blanchette

18. *The Tooth of Crime* by Sam Shepard. Photo: Ron Blanchette

19. *Angel City* by Sam Shepard. Photo: Ron Blanchette

child, he was fascinated by puppets and school plays. On scholarship at San Jose State University, he read plays omnivorously and worked at the first of several versions of his *Shrunken Head of Pancho Villa.* While many of his family were active in the California grape strike, he continued to play at his plays – until Davis's Mime Troupe performed on the San Jose campus. Magnetized by their lively style, he joined the Troupe. When he marched with the *Huelga,* he was encouraged by United Farmworkers' President Chavez to found a farmworkers' theatre.

Armed with signs to designate *Huelgista* (striker), *Esquirol* (strikebreaker), *Patroncito* (grower), and *Contractista* (contractor), Valdez asked workers to enact these roles of their daily experience; their colleagues became audience and critics. Picketing all day, the farmworker–actors rehearsed at night and performed weekly in *actos* which Valdez wrote not merely about but for the workers. Enacting daily union events, the skits could be in Spanish, English, or the mixture called Spanglish. Sometimes actors played at union headquarters in Delano, California, but more often on the flatbed of a truck driven right up to the picket line. By 1966, the troupe performed *actos* in many towns between Delano and the state capital in Sacramento, finding an audience even outside the Chicano community.

The union won its strike, and in 1976 El Teatro Campesino travelled across the country, playing union halls and more commercial venues. Back in California, Valdez moved his company away from union headquarters to establish *El Centro Campesino Culturál* for the fostering of Chicano pride in their cultural heritage. By 1968 other Chicano theatre groups sprang up in southwestern United States and Latin America, forming TENAZ, *Teatro Nacionál de Aztlan*, with annual festivals and an irregularly published periodical. In 1970 the *Centro* bought forty acres in the California mission town of San Juan Bautista, where they work culturally and agriculturally as an economic collective, and where construction of a theatre is projected for 1982.

As with the Living Theatre and the San Francisco Mime Troup, El Teatro Campesino starts a new work with collective discussion, but *actos* started with discussions based on the day's picketing. Valdez early codified the method: 'Inspire the audience to social action. Illuminate specific points and social problems. Satirize the opposition. Show or hint at a solution.' Gradually, the *actos* became more sophisticated; signs were replaced by masks and skilled physicality; solutions were not always evident.

In 1971 El Teatro Campesino published a volume of nine *actos* written between 1965 and 1971 by 'Luis Valdez y el Teatro Campesino', Valdez relinquishing his anonymity. Of the nine, only three deal with farm labour problems. Two examine the problematic role of Chicanos in the Viet War. A puppet play portrays Aztec history of Mexico, and three plays deal with La Raza in a way that predicts the new form of *mito*, or dramatization of Aztec and Mayan myths.

The only transplant from the 1965 picket line is *Las Dos Caras del Patroncito* (The Two Faces of the Boss). Basically a vaudeville skit in which the Boss and the farmworker exchange clothes and attitudes, it points out that attitude is locked into social class. When the Campesino dons the Boss's clothes – including the pigmask that became traditional for that character – he also dons a redneck viewpoint: 'I don't pay you to think son. I pay you to work.' Momentarily at least, the Boss in Campesino clothes realizes: 'You know that damn Caesar Chavez is right? You can't do this work for less than two dollars an hour.'

La Quinta Temporada (The Fifth Season – 1966) is more sustained. A farmworker, exploited both by Boss and

Contractor, lives precariously through the four seasons, personified by actors. Summer is dressed like an ordinary farmworker, but his clothes are covered with paper money. Fall is also covered with money, but more sparsely. Winter is a monster who seizes money from everyone in sight. Spring rescues the mistreated farmworker, indoctrinates him with union slogans, but disappears all too soon. By the time Summer and Fall reappear with their temptations, the farmworker has gone on strike. Winter then attacks the Grower, who is rescued only when he consents to a union contract. Winter's sign gives way to that of the fifth season – social justice.

One of the most popular *actos* on university campuses is *Los Vendidos* (The Sell-outs – 1967). Miss Jimenez of the State Government shops in Honest Sancho's Used Mexican Lot for a token brown face to display in government offices. She rejects a Farmworker who shouts 'Huelga', a *Pachuco* (city slicker) who steals, a Revolutionary who is made in Mexico, in favour of a Mexican-American who snaps to her commands. But this purchase breaks down, so that he unexpectedly incites his fellow-Mexicans to revolution. 'The three models join together and advance toward the secretary who backs up and runs out of the shop screaming.' Relieving 'Honest' Sancho of his profit, the three are not sell-outs, and they go to a party. (This *acto* was televised nationally.)

The longest *acto* in the collection, *No Saco Nada de la Escuela* (I Don't Get Anything Out of School – 1969) traces Black, white, and Chicano students through three stages of school – elementary, high, and university, to show that Anglo education educates for an Anglo world. Similarly, the Vietnam *actos* show the folly of Chicano soldiers fighting for Anglo superiority.

Soldado Razo (Chicano Soldier – 1971) prefigures the

Mime Troupe's Washington Jefferson of *False Promises*.
Both are naïve Third World characters who volunteer for
duty in an imperialist American Army. Both learn first
hand of the brutalities expected of them, and both revolt –
too late. Dramaturgically, both plays stray from the comic
norm of their respective playwrights. *Soldado Razo* opens
with Chicano Johnny's death in Vietnam, and moves
through flashback scenes linked by the visible presence of
Death as a character. That figure darkens Johnny's pre-war
exchanges with family and fiancée. Johnny is killed before
he can reveal the full horror of the Viet War; his body is
shipped home, and a pensive family in mourning files past
his bier, questioning the need for such death. Although
grouped with the *actos, Soldado Razo* indicates the path of
Valdez's *mitos*, no longer agit-prop.

Few of the *mitos* have as yet been published, but *The
Dark Root of A Scream* not only illustrates the form;
following *Soldado Razo*, it shows the continuity of Valdez's
evolution. The *acto* is a flashback series from a death in
Vietnam; the *mito* is an emblematic spectrum of reactions
to a death in Vietnam. Both plays implicitly decry Chicano
acceptance of their sacrificial role. Death is the only
non-realistic character of the *acto*, whereas the *mito* is
rooted in transcendence for its dead hero, significantly
named Quetzalcoatl Gonzales, a blend of native Mexican
and Spanish heritage. As opposed to the summary disposi-
tion of Johnny's body in the *acto*, the coffin of Quetzalcoatl
Gonzales is set aloft on a pyramid 'with the most real
artifacts of *barrio* life at the broad base and an abstract
mythical-religious peak at the top.' The stage action moves
back and forth between *Pachucos* on a street corner and a
family at a wake. The reactions to the Vietnam death of
Quetzalcoatl Gonzales range across the facile clichés of a
priest, his mother's grief, the Chicano pride he has taught

to Conejo and his sister Dalia, the cynicism of the *Pachucos* in the *barrio*. At the play's climax, the coffin bleeds through the American flag, and when the mother looks in, there is the green feathered headdress of the god Quetzalcoatl. At the last, all are awed by the beating heart found in the coffin: 'The heart gives out light in the descending darkness', symbolizing a mythic redemption.

What *acto* and *mito* both reject is the European heritage of proscenium theatre. In Valdez's words: 'Our rejection of white western European *(gavacho)* proscenium theatre makes the birth of new Chicano forms necessary – thus, *los actos y los mitos*; one through the eyes of man; the other, through the eyes of God.' Since it is the specific man Valdez who pens the *mitos* ostensibly 'through the eyes of God', he has met with adverse criticism both in and outside the Chicano community, charged with betraying his radical stance. This charge has been levelled, too, against his latest form patterned on the *corrido* or musical epic of sixteenth-century Spain, but containing many modern musical forms. It is hard to tell from a single viewing whether these performances are musical comedy, where music is the primary ingredient, or drama with musical interludes. It is even possible that the two best-known recent productions of El Teatro Campesino do not belong to the same genre.

Mundo is described by Valdez as a Chicano Mystery/ Miracle Play. It was conceived in 1972 and slowly developed for performance in 1975 on the Mexican Day of the Dead. After four main revisions, it is still touring widely, but it has not been published. The story concerns Mundo Mata, a *barrio* Chicano, who dies of a drug overdose and sets out through the underworld in search of his pregnant wife, his grandparents, and his friends. He relives incidents in the life of a *barrio* Chicano – dances, cruising, knife fights, holdups, receipt of welfare, freeway accident. He pleads with powerful men in the U.S. and the U.S.S.R., who are indifferent to his plight. Through music and dance the dead Mundo returns to life in a resurrection motif that is basic to the pre-Columbian Indians to whom the Chicanos trace their heritage.

Zoot Suit (1978), commissioned by Gordon Davidson for the Los Angeles Mark Taper Forum, is based on an actual event, when American soldiers were sent in 1943 to quell 'zoot-suit' riots in the Los Angeles *barrio*. An Anglo court condemned seventeen Mexican-Americans to life imprisonment on a false murder charge. The case was appealed and won on the basis of evidence from Communist reporter Alice Bloomfield. Like fictional Mundo, the 'factual' defendant Henry Reyna undertakes a musical odyssey through the *barrio*. Tempted and assailed, he ends in a triumph that has attracted both Anglo and Chicano audiences in Los Angeles, but not on Broadway. It may say more about the 1970s than about radical theatre that Ronnie Davis, founder but no longer member of the San Francisco Mime Troupe – to which Valdez also belonged – has condemned *Zoot Suit* as the climax of Valdez's idealization of the *pachuco* – begun in Valdez's *Shrunken Head of Pancho Villa*, strengthened in *The Dark Root of The Scream*, and crystallized in the sympathetic characters of Mundo and Reyna. No one, however, can condemn the radical accomplishments of Valdez in the context of the Chicano theatre movement.

In contrast to Britain, where political radicals dominate recent dramaturgy, such playwrights have received small subsidy in the United States. The Becks have written phrases to speak, rather than plays, as an adjunct to their main activity of anarchizing through theatre. Joan Holden continues to adapt popular genres for radical causes – local to global – espoused by the San Francisco Mime Troupe.

The Becks, Holden, Valdez

Luis Valdez has distinguished the 1960s from the 1970s as a time for outward explosion changed to a time for inward implosion. Will there be explosion at all in the 1980s?

6
Black on Black:
Baraka, Bullins,
Kennedy

When the word 'Black' dislodged 'Negro', a radical self-examination was forced upon the United States – reflected in theatre. Loraine Hansberry's 1959 *Raisin in the Sun* seemed to hold promise for Negro playwrights as well as actors; her cast included actor/playwrights Ossie Davis, Lonne Elder, Douglas Turner Ward. Only two years later Jean Genet's *The Blacks* exploded Off-Broadway, with then-unknown performers who have since attained celebrity – Roscoe Lee Browne, Godfrey Cambridge, Charles Gordone, James Earl Jones, Cicely Tyson. By the end of the three-year run of *The Blacks* (with cast replacements), Genet's fury inflamed the early days of LeRoi Jones, and the Negro Ensemble Company was founded and funded.

Blacks were united in racial pride and purpose, so long denied them by whites. In a Black drama anthology of 1970 theatremen Woodie King and Ron Milner urged: 'Black theater – go home!' By home they meant the urban ghetto. In Harlem, Newark, Detroit, Chicago, San Francisco, theatres were borne on the shoulders of a few indefatigable Black workers, but none of them lasted as long as the subsidized Negro Ensemble Company. At the end of the 1960s Doris Abramson concluded her study of Negro drama: 'Negro playwrights are in the same position today that they were in yesterday. They must find patronage where they can and, having found it, present plays about Negroes to a predominantly white audience whose values their plays frequently attack.' Substitute the word 'Black' for 'Negro', and the statement holds true for 1980. With the exception of brave, short-lived theatres in the Black ghetto, Black dramatists have continued to entertain predominantly white audiences whose values engulf them. Black playwrights find it harder than whites to survive in unsubsidized theatres; there is small middle-class support, and theatre is scarcely a necessity among those living marginally. And yet there is a generation of elder Black playwrights – James Baldwin, Alice Childress, the late Langston Hughes, Loften Mitchell, Ted Shine, as well as younger voices of Ben Caldwell, Philip Hayes Dean Charles Gordone, Paul Carter Harrison, Richard Wesley, Edgar White. Three Black playwrights, for whom Blackness is an obsessive theme, have written memorable plays in the last two decades – Amiri Baraka, Ed Bullins, and Adrienne Kennedy.

Amiri Baraka has been a beacon to his people. Black critic Kimberly Benston claims: 'Baraka entered the American consciousness not merely as a writer but as an event.' Born Everett Leroi Jones in 1934, he early rebelled against his middle-class Newark environment. At Howard University he valued only the teaching of poet Sterling Brown and sociologist E. Franklin Frazier. He dropped out of the university to enlist in the Air Force, where he read voraciously. At the end of his two-year tour of duty, he reacted against order by plunging into the Bohemianism of Greenwich Village, where he began to write in different genres. Since then, he has undergone several changes of belief and expression. Werner Sollors's study provides a helpful chronology:

	1958–61	1960–5	1964–74	1974–
Commitment	aesthetic protest	political/ ethnic protest	Black Cultural Nationalism	Marxism Leninism Mao-Tse-Tung-Thought
	Beat Bohemianism	New left	Kawaida	
Aesthetic	expressive	mimetic	pragmatic	pragmatic

In each of these periods Baraka wrote plays, but his earliest endeavours are lost.

The Eighth Ditch (Is Drama) (1960) was later incorporated into his novel *The System of Dante's Inferno.* The Florentine poet consigned false counsellors to the eighth ditch of his eighth infernal circle, and Baraka's false counsellor has a number instead of a name – 64 or 8 × 8. A seduction/rape of 46 by 64, *Eighth Ditch* seeks to shock by subject and language. Baraka has dismissed the play as 'foetus drama', and Sollors interprets it as two aspects of Baraka himself – the adolescent bourgeois 46 raped by the ghetto Black 64. Published in a literary quarterly before it was produced by an Off-Off-Broadway Poets' Theatre, *Eighth Ditch* initiated Baraka into conflict with the law. The periodical was confiscated, the Poets' Theatre was fined, and Baraka defended himself in court – successfully. The experience spurred him to new shock tactics. Blasphemy, obscenity, iconoclasm are omnipresent in Baraka's four plays which gained him notoriety when they were performed in New York in 1964 – *The Baptism, The Toilet, Dutchman,* and *The Slave.*

Set in a Black Baptist church, *The Baptism* is sacrilegious. A Minister and a Bohemian homosexual vie for the favours of an adolescent Boy seeking baptism. An Old Woman accuses the Boy of the sin of masturbation, but six girls worship him as the 'beautiful screw of the universe', then turn against him, lusting for a second crucifixion. Only the Homosexual objects to their attack, but he is easily conquered. The Boy slays his enemies with a silver sword, but a motorcycle Messenger summons him to his father, who is about to destroy the world 'as soon as the bars let out'. Refusing to forsake erring humanity, the Boy is knocked unconscious, to be carried off by the Messenger. The Homosexual regains consciousness and wonders: 'What happened to that cute little religious fanatic?' When the play ends, the audience wonders too. A masturbating, murdering Christ-analogue; sexually repressed and repressive Christians; a sardonic Homosexual who cruises bars and churches; a divine messenger in the form of a Hell's angel; a titular baptism, a silver sword, and a hint of a Holy Grail – the details do not cohere into mere burlesque or serious apocalypse.

Continuing his infernal travels, Baraka entitles his next play for its setting; 'The Toilet' is a stinking high-school latrine in which the characters excrete literally and symbolically. A duel takes place there between white James Karolis and Black Ray Foots. When Karolis gains a choke hold on Foots, Blacks enter the fray, punch Karolis unconscious, and leave him inert. But Ray returns and cradles in his arms the head of his beloved enemy. The hero's name hints at Baraka's own ambivalence – the light Ray of love and the grounded Foots of Macho pressure.

In the original production of *The Toilet* young actors orchestrated the ghetto obscenities. In Larry Rivers's sculpted latrine the adolescents jabbed, swore, pivoted, taunted, and collectively rose to an orgiastic riot. With an educational institution reduced to excrement, with sporting spirit crumbled to cruelty, with colour reversal for a lynch mob, *The Toilet* does not fit the love story to the race story. Memorable, however, is a final tender image of Black arms cradling a white head in a contemporary Pietà.

Tenderness is mortally wounded in *Dutchman,* the drama that made Baraka famous when he was still Leroi Jones. The subway in summer – what Baraka describes as 'the flying underbelly of the city' – is his most telling dramatic inferno. A sober seated passenger is first seen in this speeding carrier. When it stops, he exchanges glances with a woman outside. When it starts up again, the woman enters the car – a beautiful, scantily dressed white woman, eating an apple. She chooses a seat beside the well-dressed young Black, accuses him of staring at her, and admits seeking him out. Lula banters with Clay before an abrupt racial taunt: 'I bet you never once thought you were a black nigger.' By the next act, the rest of the subway car is visible, the two are physically touching, and the flirtation takes the form of Lula's 'chronicle' of the evening ahead of them. As more passengers enter the car, Lula's actions grow manic. embarrassing Clay. She sings, twists, dances, and tries to make him dance with her. When he attempts to restrain her, she insults him: 'Screw yourself, Uncle Tom. Thomas Woolly-head.' While passengers laugh, Clay clubs a drunk, forces Lula to her seat, and slaps her twice. He has shed his respectable carapace, and he launches into a monologue of rage.

The theme of his speech is that Blacks are forever unknowable to whites. His own Ivy League appearance and the art of Bessie Smith and Charlie Parker are sublimations of murderous emotion. The day of reckoning will come; just when the Black man appears most integrated, he will be most deadly: 'They'll cut your throats, and drag you out to the edge of your cities so the flesh can fall away from your bones, in sanitary isolation.' Lula says she has 'heard enough', and when Clay bends over her to claim his belongings, she stabs him twice. Following her orders, the other passengers drag Clay's body out. Another young Black enters, books under his arm, and sits a few seats behind Lula. They exchange looks.

Dutchman has been published with two endings. In the original Apollo edition a Negro conductor shuffles down the subway aisle and greets the young Black: 'Hey, brother', who responds, 'Hey'. Black men recognize their fraternity, despite costumes. In the version published by Edward Parone, the play's first director, there is no conductor, but Lula nibbles an apple after sizing up her new victim.

The brilliance of *Dutchman* lies in a fusion of symbolism and realism. Act I catches the interracial banter of Bohemians. The setting, however, suggest the mythic, which is confirmed by the characters' names; the young Black is clay in the hands of the Lulu-Lilith white woman, *la belle dame sans merci*. Thus prepared, Act II bursts out of psychological probability into myth – Black against white, man against woman, private emotions against public spectacle. As Sherley Anne Williams showed, Baraka anchors his play in three myths: (1) 'the *Flying Dutchman* . . . roamed the seas and added unwary ships to its phantom entourage'; (2) 'a Dutch man-of-war . . . brought the first Black slaves to North America'; and (3) 'the apples . . . seem to bear some resemblance to the biblical fruit of the tree of knowledge'. The white seductress tempts the slave's scion to self-knowledge, but with that knowledge comes death, and the ritual temptation-murder will be repeated eternally.

Of Baraka's four infernoes of 1964, *The Slave* alone

dramatizes an Inferno of the Black protagonist's own making. Walker Vessels, a Black leader in a race war, returns to the home of his white ex-wife and her liberal husband, formerly his literature professor. As the outside war draws closer, the three insult one another, Walker drinking heavily. When the professor attempts to over-power Walker, the latter shoots him. Walker's wife Grace is fatally injured in an explosion, and he lets her die in the belief that their children are dead, but a child's screams are the last sounds before a final explosion.

Baraka later grouped Vessels with Clay and Foots as victims, but in the play he is the controlling agent. What Baraka and most critics forget is the play's beginning and end, where Vessels appears as an old field slave. The half-senile old man contradicts the revolutionary assurance of the race-proud killer. In the body of the play drama is diluted into discussion, for all the background explosions. *The Slave* may have served Baraka's transition to Black nationalism, but dramatically it is drained of energy.

In 1967 Leroi Jones became Imamu Amiri Baraka, a minister of the Kawaida faith. He then founded Spirit House, but his agit-prop plays predate the conversion. As men-tioned in chapter 5, agit-prop tends to employ either shock techniques or broad satire. Baraka's plays shock. His anti-white rage flails out for a dramatic style. *Experimental Death Unit #1* (1965) begins as an Absurdist dialogue between two white hopheads vying for a Black whore, but the titular Black execution squad slays all three, mounting the white heads on pikes. *A Black Mass* (1966) is science fiction; Jacoub in the laboratory manufactures a white beast whose evil progeny are rampant in today's world. *Great Goodness of Life* (1969) (dedicated 'with love and respect' to his father) is the expressionist trial of Court Royal, who longs for the great goodness of life as lived by white middle-class America, and who therefore follows the commands of a mysterious Voice. After killing his Black Nationalist son, he is free to go bowling. *Madheart* (1967) is a morality play in which a Black Everyman moves past female obstacles – a white Devil Lady, an Uncle Tom mother, an assimilationist sister, and an independent Black Woman, whom he subdues to his will. *Jello* (1965) is a burlesque of the Jello-sponsored Jack Benny show, in which the Black servant Rochester rises up against his white employers. *Bloodrites* (1970) is a dance drama in which a Black chorus exorcize white devils of the mass media, enabling them to raise a Black man from the ground.

Slave Ship (1967) is subtitled 'A Historical Pageant'. Subduing his verbal flow, Baraka relies upon music to support his images of Black history: the proud native Africans, the chained slaves bound for America, the auction block and family dispersal, the seeds of revolt, modern Christian hypocrisy and African sensibility, and the final chant of Afro-American revolutionary power. Although the pageant ends in a celebration with Black audience participation, the head of the time-serving minister is rolled into their midst, and actual performances closed with anti-white chants. Kimberly Benston has described Baraka's dramatic development: 'The tragedy-burdened slave ship of *Dutchman* has become the dance-filled celebration of *Slave Ship;* musical transcendence has risen from the spirit of tragedy.'

In 1974 Baraka renounced Black Nationalism for international Marxist–Leninist–Maoist Thought, and his writing has become didactic. *S–1* and *The Motion of History* (1976) recall left-wing theatre of the 1930s, except that the protagonists are Black. Allowing for the significance of this difference, one nevertheless finds it hard to imagine that

101

these plays will convince anyone but the convinced – especially since they are alleviated by none of the humour that enhances the works of radical playwrights Holden or Valdez.

'S–1' stands for the Congressional bill that virtually legalizes Fascism in the United States. Despite a few quivering liberals, the bill becomes law, and a Black Communist couple are victimized. A newspaperman ignores the admonishments of his publisher and consents to be educated by the Blacks, helping expose Fascism. The play closes with the wife's ringing prediction of people's victory – broadcast illegally. More colourful, *The Motion of History* recapitulates some of the material of *Slave Ship,* but history narrows down to Richie and Lennie, modern 'white and Black dudes', who gradually renounce Bohemia for commitment to workers' revolution. The dramatic energy that drove Baraka's earlier styles has subsided to pulpit didacticism in a very different religion from his clergyman forefathers. But Baraka is not yet fifty, and new dramatic power may yet grow from his new faith.

Born within a few hundred miles and a few months (in 1934) of one another, Leroi Jones and Ed Bullins entered different worlds – the Black bourgeoisie as opposed to the Black ghetto. Bullins has said that all the men of his family belong to the criminal class; he was the first to attend high school, but he dropped out. Jones joined the Air Force in reaction against the university, but Bullins joined the Navy after living from hand to mouth. Yet both young Blacks managed to read insatiably during their enlistments. After his military stint, Bullins went back to school, acquiring a high-school diploma. He drifted Westward to Los Angeles and enrolled in writing courses at Los Angeles City College, then moved North to San Francisco State University. Like Baraka, Bullins began to write verse, essays, fiction, as well as drama: 'I turned to writing plays because I found that the people I was interested in writing about or writing to – my people – didn't read much fiction, essays, or poetry.' Unsaid is the sad fact that his people do not see many plays either. Bullins and a few friends produced his first plays in the Off-Off-Broadway of San Francisco, where he became for a short time Minister of Culture for the Black Panthers. When Robert Macbeth of Harlem's New Lafayette Theatre sent him a plane ticket, Bullins flew East and made that theatre his home from 1967 to 1972. As prolific as Baraka, Bullins has not yet received that writer's critical attention, but Joe Papp has provided him with productions at New York's Public Theatre.

Bullins's first plays date from 1965, sometimes dramatizing his fiction and usually satirizing Black bourgeois life. The title of his first play – *How Do You Do* – is a stereotypical bourgeois greeting that becomes a rhythmic refrain. Paul, an 'image-maker', ponders Roger and Dora Stereotype as they transform through several cliché Black roles – refined intellectuals, conspicuous consumers, sex objects for whites, lust-filled ne'er-do-wells, integrationist liberals. Having witnessed these avatars, Paul begins to write: 'How do you do?' A more sustained satire of Black intellectuals is the widely anthologized *Electronic Nigger* (1968), with its shocking and self-explanatory title.

In his first year of dramatic writing, Bullins drew upon his familiarity with Black lower depths for *Clara's Ole Man* (1965). In a Philadelphia slum eighteen-year-old Clara has invited Jack of the Ivy League suit and diction to visit her 'in the afternoon when her ole man would be at work'. Jack finds that Clara lives with Baby Girl and Big Girl. Enter three sixteen-year-olds who have robbed an old man; they are quickly subdued by Big Girl. After much wine, Big Girl takes Clara to the show to which Jack has invited her, and the young toughs take Jack outside to beat him up – on prior order of Big Girl, who is Clara's ole man.

A volume of *Four Dynamite Plays* (1971) resembles Baraka's revolutionary plays – short, simplistic, filled with anti-white obscenities. *It Bees That Way* (1970) is Bullins's version of 'Offending the Audience', with slum Blacks turning upon their white audience. In *Death List* (1970) a Black revolutionary lists for execution actual Blacks who supported the state of Israel. (The entire collection is dedicated to Al-Fatah.) *Pig Pen* (1970) paints a miscellaneous group of Bohemian Blacks, upon whom the assassination of Malcolm X has little effect. *Night of the Beast* (1970) is a film script about a Black/white civil war, with victory to the Blacks.

In his most telling plays Bullins dramatizes the Black urban ghetto. He prefaces his first collection with a quotation from Baraka: 'All their faces turned into the lights and you work on them black nigger magic, and cleanse them at having seen the ugliness and if the beautiful sees themselves, they will love themselves.' Bullins keeps the beautiful all but invisible, although there is beautiful dignity buried far below the religious mother's orthodoxy in *A Son, Come Home* (1968). Most of his plays, however, dramatize the ugliness of Black ghetto life; his characters are thieves, pimps, prostitutes, drug pushers, and yet they have spirit and humour. Like Chekhov, Bullins probes the faults of his people to 'cleanse them at having seen the ugliness'.

In the mid-1960s Bullins began work on a cycle of twenty plays about Afro-Americans between 1900 and 1999, but he has continued to write plays outside the cycle too. Perhaps the most cheerily chilling of the latter group is *Goin' a Buffalo* (1968). Like Chekhov's Three Sisters who dream of going to Moscow, Bullins's pimps and whores dream of escaping from Los Angeles to Buffalo: 'I heard that Buffalo is really boss.' Through death and betrayal, the dream approaches reality. One Black betrays his friend, annexes his Black and white molls, and orders the women to pack. When asked where they are going, he replies, to close the play: 'To Buffalo, baby. Where else?' Ruthlessness and ingenuity are the only ways to dream-fulfilment.

Another extra-cycle play was commissioned by Gordon Davidson for the Mark Taper Forum – *The Taking of Miss Janie* (1975). The play opens with a brutal 'taking of [white] Miss Janie' by rape. An extended flashback reveals how the white woman and Black man met at school in the hip scene of the 1960s; only the Black Nationalist rages against easy integration. One Black–white marriage survives in spite of friction, a Black woman becomes a lesbian after two marriages (one to the protagonist Monty), another Black woman slips easily into anyone's bed, two Jewish men diverge into drug addict and Bahai addict. By the end of the play Monty offers love to Miss Janie, in the form of more sexual pleasure than she has ever known – or so he promises. In spite of its anti-Semitism, the play won the 1975 New York Drama Critics Circle Award, but Bullins worried about poor attendance: 'Maybe the whites are threatened and the niggers are embarrassed.' Maybe indeed.

The plays of Bullins's Afro-American cycle lend each other strength. They are not being written in chronological order, and they are linked not by plot but by characters weaving through separate plays. What seems to be the first chronologically is one of the last to be written, *Home Boy* (1976). Unusual for Bullins is the small-town Southern setting for two young friends, Jody and Dude. The latter soon escapes to a Northern city where he learns stealing, whoring, dope dealing, and, in his words, 'revoltin' and revolutionin'.'

Although Bullins no longer mentions the one-act *Corner* (1969) as part of his cycle, it offers a first view of Cliff Dawson, one of the cycle's protagonists. Set on a Los Angeles street corner in the 1950s, it sketches young ghetto Blacks who spend aimless days drinking, stealing, fornicating. Drunk and desultorily flirting with Cliff's girl Stella, the young Blacks taunt one another with sharp wit. When the acknowledged leader Cliff arrives, he parks a drunken Stella in a broken-down car for a gang rape. He confesses to his friend Bummie that he has impregnated Lou, who has been supporting him: 'You can start callin' me Daddy Cliff.' *In The Wine Time* (1968) shows Cliff's ménage, a perpetual wine time for Cliff and Lou's fifteen-year-old nephew. Cliff lives on pregnant Lou's earnings while he drinks and whores. When nephew Ray stabs another teenager, Cliff takes the blame, so that the teenager can avoid prison. *In New England Winter* (1967) finds Cliff after seven years in prison. His half-brother Steve Benson masterminds a robbery in order to rejoin an old love in New England in winter. The play intercuts 1955 New England scenes with the 1960 robbery rehearsal – a four-man rehearsal demanding disguise and precise timing. Intellectual Steve cuts his friend Bummie's throat to prevent the revelation of a Steve–Lou love affair during Cliff's imprisonment: 'But it was for nothing, Steve . . . I knew.' With Bummie dead, three men successfully perform the robbery.

The Duplex (1970) houses Steve in Los Angeles during the 1960s. A sometime student, he shares his top-floor flat with Marco Polo Henderson. The first-floor flat is occupied by the duplex owner Velma, married to brutal O.D., but loved by Steve, who has apparently not gone to New England. The duplex is the locale of pointless pleasures – cards, wine, marijuana, adultery. The play's subtitle 'A

Black Love Fable in Four Movements' signals Steve's two approaches toward and retreats from Velma. After Steve is nearly killed by Velma's husband, and Velma is clearly victimized by his violence, old Montgomery Henderson breezes innocently into the duplex to conclude the play: 'Hey, ev'va body! Grab yo cards, whiskey 'n' women! It's party time!'

In *The Fabulous Miss Marie* (1970) it is always party time; that is why Miss Marie (Steve's occasional mistress in the preceding play) is fabulous. Daughter of a university graduate, granddaughter of a schoolteacher, Marie when pregnant married dancer Bill Horton who brought her to Los Angeles where he parks cars for 'two hundred stone cold dollars a week . . . . We make almost as much as some colored doctors make . . . 'n we spend it too. 'Cause it's party time every day at Miss Marie's house.' Miss Marie's Christmas party guests proclaim that they are having a good time, but boredom seeps through the tired language of schoolteacher, social worker, dress designer. Bullins's Black bourgeoisie lacks the vigour and invention of his ghetto criminals. Like Chekhov's dying aristocrats, Bullins's anachronistic bourgeois indulge themselves in a world that is passing them by. Steve Benson, once an intellectual, is finally detained by fabulous Miss Marie to join her in a perpetual party.

Bullins has produced no single play as powerful as Baraka's *Dutchman,* but he is a more consistent dramatic craftsman. Evident both in and outside of the cycle are his sharp command of the *humour* of Black colloquial speech, an ear attuned to its rhythms, and a lack of inhibition about its lyricism. Although he wavers politically, Bullins's most accomplished plays present a tragi-comic picture of Black vigour and courage, against overwhelming odds.

As Baraka and Bullins approach the age of fifty, they

both seek wide audiences for their plays of Afro-American experience, but for different reasons. Baraka is a convert to Marxist Maoism, whereas Bullins is 'investigating the idea that Marxism is a Zionist conspiracy'. For Baraka, writing is an instrument toward a life-pattern, and his recent plays deal discursively with revolutionary pattern. Bullins, one-time Cultural Minister for the Black Panthers, seems disenchanted with politics and determined to make his writing 'the central activity, the mainstay, the source, the wellspring, the guiding tenet'. For younger Black play-wrights seeking role-models, this divergence may clarify the issue. Or may confuse it.

It is rare to find a sympathetic woman in the dramas of Baraka or Bullins. Passive supporters of their Black mates or whimpering whites recur in Baraka's plays; to these stereotypes Bullins adds the domineering lesbian Big Girl and perpetual party-goers like the fabulous Miss Marie. Baraka and Bullins dramatize the new Black *male* consciousness, but Adrienne Kennedy stages her own Black and lyrical *un*conscious: 'I see my writing as being an outlet for inner, psychological confusion and questions stemming from childhood . . . . You try to struggle with the material that is lodged in your unconscious, and try to bring it to the conscious level.'

In early background, Kennedy is closer to Baraka than to Bullins. Born in 1931 in Pittsburgh into a middle-class Black family, she was brought up in a mixed neighbour-hood in Cleveland. Like Baraka, she went to the univer-sity, and like him, she dropped out because her studies seemed irrelevant to her life. Like Baraka, too, she was drawn to the avant-garde of New York City in the early 1960s, but her plays differ from any of his styles. Describing her plays as 'states of mind', she does herself theatrical injustice. Her plays are *acts* of mind – tremulous or masterful, but always highly imaged and eloquent.

In a Playwrights' Workshop conducted by Edward Albee she wrote *Funnyhouse of a Negro* (1962), which won an Obie in 1964. Often cited as her best work, this drama announces her main style, sometimes called surrealist and sometimes expressionist, and actually a delicate blend of aspects of both. Kennedy's plays are expressionist in their subjectivity, with inner conflicts externalized as different characters; they are surrealist in their close dependence on dreams with strong visual images. They are original in the particular images and in the incantatory repetitions that extend the subjective into the mythic.

Funnyhouse of a Negro is both setting and metaphor for the dwelling of Negro Sarah. The play's characters are divided into white and coloured, but the division shifts subtly. Sarah is the titular Negro, whose 'funnyhouse' is dominated by a white landlady and a Jewish lover. Sarah's light-skinned mother looks white, and Sarah herself is the product of her Black father's rape of her mother. Torn between the two strands of her heritage, Sarah is seen and heard through four selves – white Queen Victoria and Duchess of Hapsburg, Black Patrice Lumumba, and yellow hunchbacked Jesus. Through the speech of all four selves runs the motif of her Black father, whose search for identity is transmitted to his daughter. A dark man, he disappoints his mother by marrying Sarah's light mother whom he then drives mad by taking her to Africa to engage in missionary work. His Black spirit duels with his yellow-skinned daughter who is haunted by his suicide after the murder of Lumumba. When Sarah's several selves fragment and repeat one another, 'her father's black figures with bludgeoned hands rush upon her, the lights black and we see her hanging in the room.' The white landlady repeats Sarah's account of her father's Harlem hanging after

Lumumba's murder, but the white poet ends the play in denial: 'Her father is a nigger who eats his meals on a white glass table.' There is neither truth nor rest for the perturbed spirits in the white funnyhouse of a Negro.

This summary arranges Kennedy's scenes into a rationality that is poetically denied by her visual and verbal imagination. In the opening mime, for example, a wild-haired woman in white mask and nightgown walks dreaming across the stage, carrying a bald head. The Queen and Duchess wear identical cheap white gowns and headpieces from which frizzy hair shows, and they talk about their dead Black father who keeps returning to the house. The Negro Sarah is dressed in black, with a rope around her neck, and she is frightened by her lack of self-awareness:

> My friends will be white. I need them as an embankment to keep me from reflecting too much upon the fact that I am a Negro. For, like all educated Negroes – out of life and death essential – I find it necessary to maintain a stark fortress against recognition for myself . . . . The characters are myself: the Duchess of Hapsburg, Queen Victoria Regina, Jesus, Patrice Lumumba. The rooms are my rooms; a Hapsburg chamber, a chamber in a Victorian castle, the hotel where I killed my father, the jungle . . . . I find there are no places, only my funnyhouse.

As in a funnyhouse, Kennedy's figures change shape, distortedly mirroring one another. As Patrice Lumumba, she half-repeats what she said as the Negro: 'My friends will be white. I need them as an embankment to keep me from reflecting too much upon the fact that I am Patrice Lumumba who haunted my mother's conception.'

110

Throughout the play Kennedy bases striking scenes on hair – baldness, wild straight hair, frizzy hair, hair torn out in patches, a nimbus on African heads. A traditional fertility symbol becomes a torture chamber. The play circles back to its beginning, with a Black man knocking at the door and a Negro woman hanging in her funnyhouse.

The Owl Answers (1963) continues the distinctive expressionist/surrealist idiom forged by Kennedy. Again the woman protagonist has several *alter egos,* formulaically repeated: 'She who is Clara Passmore, who is the Virgin Mary who is the Bastard who is the Owl.' Set in the subway, like *Dutchman,* the play also reaches for myth. The subway is explicitly equated with 'the Tower of London is a Harlem Hotel Room is St Peter's', and from scene to scene the whole set moves to show these facets. Other than the protagonist, a Black mother and white father shift identities as they 'change slowly back and forth into and out of themselves'. As Sarah of *Funnyhouse* is torn between English culture and the split strands of her Black heritage, so the protagonist She is fragmented between Clara Passmore, the Virgin, a Bastard, and an Owl, but also between her Black mother and the English literary tradition of her white Southern ancestor. She is imprisoned in the Tower of London by William the Conqueror, Anne Boleyn, and Shakespeare; at a violent moment she hears the Third Movement of Haydn's Concerto for Horn in D.

She is not only a Black woman seeking her identity in a father or the father-substitutes she lures to Harlem hotel rooms; she is also a writer who writes to her father every day, and who drops notebook pages throughout the alogical, highly imaged action. She is at once the bastard of a rich white man and his Black cook, and the schoolteacher daughter of a coloured clergyman and his wife. Shunted between Harlem and London (in circular turns of the stage subway), she knows no rest: 'I call God and the Owl answers.' In prayer, her mother stabs herself, and on the altar she tries to stab the Negro who desires her. At the last 'She who is Clara who is The Bastard who is The Virgin Mary suddenly looks like an owl, and lifts her bowed head, stares into space and speaks: "Ow . . . owww." ' Bird of traditional wisdom, Kennedy's owl cries the question 'Whoooo?' and answers in pain 'Ow . . . oww.'

Paired with *The Owl Answers* as *Cities in Bezique* (that card game coupling Queen of Spades and Jack of Diamonds), *A Beast Story* (1969) continues Kennedy's animal imagery and her fusion of expressionism and surrealism. Explicitly, the scenic directions inform us that the beasts – mother, father, and daughter – are a Black minister's family, isolated from one another in stage rooms. As in *Funnyhouse* acts of violence are repeated from generation to generation. The Beast Man rapes the Beast Woman, and a dark Human tries to rape the Beast Girl. Having poisoned their child, she smothers him: 'I have killed as she killed.' At the last, Beast Girl axes her father, a blue crow, and a giant toad: she falls weeping as beast noises grow louder. Her oblivious parents intone a harmonic ending: 'All is warm and sunlit' – in death.

The beast was a rat in *A Rat's Mass* (1966), where rathood is a metaphor for Blackness. Brother and Sister Rat are both in love with white Italian Rosemary who wears a Holy Communion dress but has worms in her hair. As She of *The Owl Answers* is magnetized to literary London, so Brother and Sister Rat are magnetized to Italian Catholicism in a time of Nazi armies. When the rat siblings intone phrases of a Rosemary who has refused to atone them, shots decimate them, and only Rosemary of the worm-hair remains.

Animal imagery is more subdued in *A Lesson in Dead*

Language (1968). The scene is an ordinary classroom. except that the teacher is a white dog 'from the waist up'. To seven little girls dressed in white she teaches a lesson in lyrical language – about bleeding that began when a white dog died. Interspersing the death of Christ, of Caesar, and of the sun, Kennedy dramatizes menstruation as a rite of admission to a classico-Christian culture. Her own favourite among her plays abjures dream images for this non-realistic classroom where the dog-teacher, the larger-than-life Roman and Christian statues, and especially the spreading red stains on white organdie theatricalize the transition from childhood to womanhood.

Like Baraka and Bullins, Kennedy has written about the murder of Malcolm X, but her play-poem *Sun* (1969) does not even mention his name. A man is in intricate interaction with differently coloured suns and moons. He is slowly dismembered as they bleed and change colour. For all the fragmentation, however, he is sensitive to cosmic rhythms, and although he is invisible at the last, his voice enunciates his vision through a small black sun.

Kennedy's *Evening with Dead Essex* (1973) is unwonted-ly realistic. Based on the assassination of Black sniper Mark James Essex, and dedicated to him and his family, the play resorts to a play within the play, but Kennedy departs further from fiction than Pirandello, Genet or even Gelber. 'The actors use their real names and the director should get the actors to play themselves.' Black actors soberly enact the life and death of their contemporary, Mark James Essex. Only the Projectionist-character is white, suggesting the surface view of a white world that murdered this idealistic young Black from the midwest. Through the actors' rehearsal, we piece together the story of a bright, church-going and obedient Black boy. During the Viet War he joined the Navy, whose racial hypocrisies unnerved him. Peace confirmed his newly dark insight into American deception toward his race. Innocent idealism backfired to murderous hate that drove him to kill racists. Late at the night rehearsal the actors enter into the spirit of dead Essex, embracing the church-going boy and the murderous hater of deception. This lone sniper was killed by over a hundred bullets, sprayed from a helicopter and two crossfires. Understanding Essex, the Black actors look at the projection of films and close their play with phrases from the Gospel of Luke: 'To heal the brokenhearted'.

Still unpublished is Kennedy's *Movie Star Has to Star in Black and White,* produced at Joe Papp's Public Theatre in 1976. Resurrecting Clara of *The Owl Answers,* Kennedy embeds her in a different white culture – no longer the English literary but the American film tradition. Leading roles are played by Bette Davis, Paul Henreid, Jean Peters, Marlon Brando, Montgomery Clift, and Shelley Winters. Supporting roles go to the expressionistically conceived Mother, Father, Husband, and a bit role to Clara herself. In a more subtle play within the play, the first scene incorporates the film *Now Voyager,* the second *Viva Zapata,* and the third *A Place in the Sun.* A prologue introduces the seamless shifts from Clara the writer to Clara, daughter of the Mother and Father, pregnant wife of Eddie, mother of Eddie Jr, and *alter ego* to any of the film actresses: 'Each day I wonder with what or with whom can I co-exist in a true union?'

Through dialogue between Bette Davis and Paul Henreid on the ocean liner from *Now Voyager* we learn of the conflict between Clara's light mother and dark father, of the disappointment of Southern Blacks when they face oppression in the North, of the strains between Clara and her husband. As in *The Owl Answers,* she calls God, and the Owl answers. She speaks through Bette Davis, of her father's wish for suicide.

The second scene merges *Viva Zapata* with a hospital in which Clara's brother Wally lies in a coma after an automobile accident. The Mother blames herself for her children's unhappiness, and through the voice of Jean Peters, Clara thinks back to *The Owl Answers* and forward to the play she hopes to write. The mutual hatred of the Father and Mother dissolves into a similar scene in *The Owl Answers*. As a small boat from *A Place in the Sun* carries Shelley Winters and Montgomery Clift to the stage, Jean Peters and Marlon Brando keep changing Clara's hospital sheets, so profusely has she bled. Eddie challenges Clara's determination to be a writer, her mother is heartbroken at their impending divorce, and her brother Wally hovers between life and death. Like Clara of *The Owl Answers,* she looks like an owl and moans 'Ow . . . oww.' Torn between her warring parents, she hears Jean Peters tell of Wally's time in an army stockade. Shelley Winters falls into the water and calls silently for help. As Montgomery Clift stares without moving, she drowns, and we hear that Wally will live with brain damaged. Family tragedy dissolves into fictional tragedy for playwright and play.

Adrienne Kennedy is that rarity – a playwright who never forces her talent. Absorbing expressionist subjectivism and surrealist dream imagery to form her own unique timbre, she has shaped the most exquisite plays of this prolific period. Whatever she writes in the future, she deserves more frequent performance of her rending dramas. Less programmatic than Baraka or Bullins, she too dramatizes the Black experience that is of deep moment. Intensely personal, her plays are contemporary renderings of the myth of the Double. Seeking an identity under schizophrenic splits, a catharsis through tragic events, the plays brim with lovely gravity.

7
From Gay to Ridiculous: Duberman, Patrick, Ludlam, Tavel, Bernard

The first anthology of gay plays, published only in 1979, classifies as gay any play 'whose central figure or figures are homosexual or one in which homosexuality is a main theme.' Editor William Hoffman pinpoints Mae West's *Drag* (1927) as the first American homosexual play. In *Drag* and *Pleasure Man* (1928) Hoffman hears a covert plea for sexual tolerance. I hear that plea also in Lillian Hellman's *Children's Hour* (1934), but Hoffman finds that she treats homosexuality 'with little lucidity'. Lucidity is not usually ascribed to Mae West (whose 1980 obituary notices ran to many other adjectives), but I have not read her plays.

Given the paucity of gay plays, some critics have dredged homosexuality from the depths of 'straight' plays, notably those of Tennessee Williams and Edward Albee. For example, Georges-Michel Sarotte in *Like a Brother, Like a Lover* states unequivocally: ' . . . our supposition *[is]* that Williams never treats heterosexuality without embodying himself in the heroine', and 'Between *The Zoo Story* and

116

Who's Afraid of Virginia Woolf? Albee wrote *The Sandbox, The American Dream*, and *The Death of Bessie Smith*. These three plays are also of assistance in confirming the basic homosexuality of Albee's work.' Such cheap psychoanalysis denies that these dramatists are superbly capable of choosing their own subjects and dramatizing them to attract audiences of all sexual persuasions.

Ignoring the sex life of playwrights, which I anachronistically believe to be his/her own affair, I devote this chapter to gay plays, and I am more inclusive than Hoffman, welcoming not only homosexual but also cross-sexual and androgynous figures. Not until the 1960s, following the lead of Blacks who addressed drama to their colleagues, did homosexual playwrights come out of the proverbial closet. It is surely by design that white homosexual historian Martin Duberman wrote his first play about the Black plight 'In White America', but analogous protests about life 'in male America' are rare, since gay playwrights tend more to literal gayness than protest.

The *O.E.D. Supplement* yields no clues as to how 'gay' came to mean homosexual, but it quotes examples from the 1950s. Duberman himself veers from the sober documentation of *In White America* to the witticisms of his gay plays, and in his latter company is Robert Patrick. Charles Ludlam, Ronald Tavel, and Kenneth Bernard call their plays 'ridiculous', which seems like a companionable adjective for 'gay'. The gay characters of these male playwrights are usually male. In William Hoffman's anthology he reports enthusiastically about the growth of gay drama and gay theatre (not always the same) in the 1960s and 1970s, but I find only five playwrights who have produced a corpus of gay plays that have been published. (One of the most prolific, Doric Wilson, is unpublished, so far as I know.)

117

Martin Duberman, born in New York City in 1930, educated through the doctorate at Ivy League schools, is a historian who writes plays. His single collection is about gayness as theme. *Male Armor* is his title for a volume of his plays written between 1968 and 1974 – a phrase based upon Wilhelm Reich's 'character armor' or 'the devices we use (which then use us) to protect ourselves from our own energy, and especially from our sexual energy'. Most of Duberman' plays are little more than sketches, rather academically analysed in his own introduction. What he calls 'evasive sparring partners' dominate a number of the plays – *Metaphors, The Recorder, The Electric Map*. Evasive though the partners may be to one another, they are quite transparent to an audience who can see through the armour to a homosexual 'pass'. In *Metaphors* a Yale University interviewer is accosted by a bright, unconventional applicant for university admission. In *Colonial Dudes* a professor and student grow progressively open to one another's language. In *The Recorder* an oral historian, armed with recorder, tries to listen in on the intimate life of the longtime companion of a deceased public figure. In *The Electric Map* two brothers, natives of history-drenched Gettysburg, respectively blame and defend their mother for the homosexuality of one of them; Duberman tries to weave the failure of the old family into the failure of the old South. *The Guttman Ordinary Scale* is a broad satire on 'scientific' sexual testing.

Of the seven plays in Duberman's collection only two are extended dramas, and for that reason perhaps, they have not been produced in an Off-Off-Broadway that prefers shorter, looser, and less comprehensive fare. *Payments* (1971) revolves around the fragile marriage of Nancy and Bob – fragile because Bob needs to break out of marriage periodically, into sex and alcohol binges. Happening to meet Sal, an old school friend who manages a call-boy service, Nancy offers him her husband's services, with a view toward obtaining financial and sexual 'payments' toward their faltering marriage. Her scheme fails, but we become spectators (voyeurs?) of Bob's initiation into the male homosexual world of New York City – witty transvestites, affluent executive, cynical journalist, brutal Marine. Each homosexual is a sociological type, and the central couple is a suburban case history; in spite of wit, violence, and costume change, the drama lacks drama.

Elagabalus (1973) is named after the third-century Roman emperor who also fascinated Artaud. Manipulating and manipulated by mother and grandmother, Elagabalus shocked Rome by his sensual self-indulgence, elevating homosexual commoners to positions of power. Duberman creates contemporary New Yorker Adrian Donner, a strikingly beautiful and wealthy young man, who poses as the Emperor Elagabalus, and leads a similar life of sensual self-indulgence. Although his mother is sympathetic to his excesses, his grandmother frowns upon them and, upon orders from her son in Washington, conspires against Adrian. The young man decides to take two simultaneous brides – his middle-aged Puerto Rican cleaning-woman and his young stable-boy lover. Over his grandmother's objections, he begins a lavish marriage ceremony: 'The results will be everything you wish. The process everything I wish.' Process and results coincide when Adrian stabs himself to death. As the other characters make twentieth-century comments, Adrian's recorded voice narrates the death of Roman Emperor Elagabalus. Adrian's faithful Puerto Rican servant places a ring on his inert finger, while his recorded voice hails the promise of a life of pleasure. Finally, the lone old woman sobs for Adrian, while a projection shows a 'teenage girl sucking sensuously on a huge popsicle'. The contemporary character, like his Roman model, died because the world was not yet ready to live for sensual pleasure.

Although Duberman's plays have met with small appreciation, he is emblematic of an American trend of the 1960s. In the radical year 1968 he strayed from history, his vocation, into drama, an avocation, using his considerable intellect and learning to decry intellect and learning – ingredients of 'male armor'. Even more anti-intellectual and anti-rational is his *Visions of Jack Kerouac* (1976), which Duberman himself describes as 'a meditation on Kerouac's life'. The play is preceded by a quotation from Allen Ginsberg's introduction to Kerouac's *Visions of Cody*, which wishes that the two friends had been 'physically tenderer' to one another. Since they have not, the play rambles through the early days of the Beats at Columbia University, their subsequent raucous encounters, their cultivation of sensual derangement, their experiments with spontaneous writing – 'Craft is crafty' – their pansexuality but Kerouac's horror of homosexuality. The implication is that Kerouac's vestigial Puritanism about homosexuality caused his disintegration through alcohol and a mother fixation. Since a current theory of history views it as fiction, Duberman exemplifies its practice – with a wistful backward glance at the sensual Beat generation.

Exemplifying theatre Off-Off-Broadway in the 1960s is Robert Patrick, its most produced playwright. His single volume of plays gives us a thumbnail biography from birth in 1937

in the shadow of somebody else's oil well in Kilgore, Texas. His childhood was spent ostensibly in many different Depression states but actually he grew up in the world-wide media mesh of slick-paper magazines, radio serials, paperback pocket books and above all before the slowly expanding screens of all-powerful Hollywood. This led him to New York, where, in 1961, he followed a Salvation Army Band to the Caffe Cino. He more or less lived there until it closed in 1968, proceeding to become, meanwhile, Off-Off-Broadway's most-produced playwright.

Emblematic is the sequence of education in the mass media (rather than school) and drift to Off-Off-Broadway. Unmentioned is the homosexuality that made Patrick *persona grata* at Caffe Cino. A self-educated actor–director–designer–technician before he became a playwright, Patrick has written over a hundred plays of which some twenty-five have been published. Only a few of these dramatize homosexuality – literally gay with a surface of glib patter, and sometimes reaching for a serious point.

Patrick's first 'Cheap Theatrick', *The Haunted Host* (1964), features a homosexual playwright haunted by the ghost of his lover who committed suicide. Enter a young lookalike of the dead lover, new to Greenwich Village and its gay scene. Most of the play consists of dialogue between 'depraved queers and simple country boys,' the country boy feeding lines to the whipping wit of the depraved queer. Punctuating the dialogue are various drug fixes and various costume changes. A seduction does not take place. The young lookalike's last words in the play are: 'I love you', and it is ambiguous as to whether the love is homosexual or brotherly. What is clear is that the declaration exorcizes the host's ghost.

One Person (1969) is again set in the gay scene of New York City. An actor's *tour de force*, it may be influenced by Lanford Wilson's *Madness of Lady Bright*. The obsessive speaker is not, however, a drag queen, but a male

121

homosexual. The 'one person' plays to invisible characters, and the play's title threads through the addresses of the speaker to his lover: 'I was one person, and you were one person, and then we – we were one person . . .' When the homosexual lovers – provisionally 'one person' – emerge into the gay bar scene, the lover goes off with someone else: 'When you see two people, walking that close together, and walking away that fast, they look – at first – like one person.'

A decade later Patrick sets *T-Shirts* (1978) in the same New York City scene. The play's three characters are a decade apart in age – forty-year-old Marvin, a playwright who loves to travel; his apartment-mate Kink, a thirty-year-old interior decorator; and handsome twenty-year-old Tom who seeks shelter in their flat on a rainy night. It is Tom who proves to be a hustler: 'Older guys have the connections and – okay – the money, and, hell, you can learn a lot from older guys.' While Tom changes into a dry T-shirt and shorts, the older men query one another, and Tom re-enters with instructions: 'First you're supposed to tell me which movie stars and great historical figures are queer.' Marvin expresses his spleen at the gay scene of the 1970s: 'Telling some kid who's having his first social success as a fist-fuckee that he's plugged into a conglomerate as heartless as Con Ed . . .' When young Tom wants to watch television, Marvin has them undress and activate a device that puts the three homosexuals on the screen. Disgusted with Tom's preening, Kink leaves to pick someone up at the baths, and Marvin departs for Rome, a pocket full of T-shirts his only luggage.

Although editor William Hoffman reads *T-Shirts* as a 'crash-course in what it's like to be a sophisticated gay man', it is rather a crash-course in what it's like to be prey to camp *bon mots*. The stage T-shirts are stamped with tired epigrams; the two older men lapse into tired comic routines, but young Tom proves more shopworn and cynical than they. Between 1964 and 1978 Patrick's handsome young stranger changed from the country boy of *Haunted Host* to a depraved queer of *T-Shirts*, but his sophisticated gay playwright brandishes the same wicked wit. Although anyone can savour such wit, it tends to attract sophisticated city audiences. In contrast, Patrick's *Kennedy's Children* (1975) has fascinated audiences in many kinds of theatre in many countries. Its five characters speak in monologues. Patrick's scenic directions specify: 'At no time do the characters relate to one another, not even at their moments of greatest duress.'

'Kennedy's children' number five, three women and two men, musing in a Lower East Side bar of New York City, like O'Neill's denizens of Harry Hope's Bar. Patrick's people are stock types of the 1960s; both men are homosexual (or bisexual) – a soldier back from Vietnam and an Off-Off-Broadway actor. One woman is a would-be sex symbol, another a former political activist, and a third has been traumatized by Kennedy's assassination with its concomitant assassination of faith in those who are 'bigger and better than other people'. Five portraits of progressive disenchantment, the monologues dovetail only in occasional references to drugs, Blacks, and the mass media – those key symbols of the 1960s. Of particular relish for theatre *aficionados* is the actor's recollection of Off-Off Broadway:

At eight o'clock, I was the left thumb in a group sensitivity demonstration called 'Hands Off' in Merrymount Episcopal Community Center, and then at ten I played a movie projector with a twinkle bulb in my mouth in a drag production of 'Bonnie and Clyde' at the Mass Dramatists Experimental Tavern, and at the stroke

123

of midnight, I was the cathectic focus of a rather tedious telepathic theatre event in the basement of the Yoga Institute. That one wasn't advertised. We all just sat together and tried to draw Clive Barnes to us with the power of prayer. I try to keep busy.

'That', as Albee's Jerry says in another context, 'is the jazz of a very special hotel', and Patrick's play aims at a larger theme – the waste of Kennedy's children without a Kennedy. Patrick has interpreted his own play (in a *Plays and Players* interview): 'The death or failure of heroes and that old ideal of the leader . . . . that's the structure of the play, its fragmentation.' A facile way of conveying fragmentation, the five monologues are mood pieces about nostalgia for heroes, but they do not probe 'that old ideal of the leader'. Although Patrick has written few explicitly gay plays, his *Kennedy's Children* profits from the casual integration of gays into the social fabric of the 1960s, a period when heroes 'died or were killed . . . . sold out or ran away' – like most periods.

Critic Stefan Brecht calls Off-Off-Broadway homosexuality 'Queer Theater', but the major practitioners – John Vaccaro, Ronald Tavel, Charles Ludlam – prefer the adjective 'ridiculous'. Director John Vaccaro and author Ronald Tavel dispute the honour of attributing that adjective to their theatres. Whoever is right, the original Play-house of the Ridiculous performed Tavel's manic word-plays under Vaccaro's manic direction. Foreseeably, the two explosive personalities parted company – in 1967 when Vaccaro, excising chunks of Tavel's *Gorilla Queen*, evidently cut him to the quick. Tavel moved his play to the Judson Poets' Theatre, and Vaccaro substituted a play by Ridiculous actor Charles Ludlam. The Vaccaro–Ludlam partnership lasted less than a year. In 1967 Vaccaro staged

Conquest of the Universe by a dissatisfied Ludlam, who thereupon withdrew to found the Ridiculous Theatrical Company. Fortuitously, Kenneth Bernard offered his plays to Vaccaro, who then directed seven Bernard plays between 1967 and 1979. Although Ludlam has stated that his theatre is an actor's theatre, Tavel's a playwright's theatre, and Vaccaro's a director's theatre, these distinctions are not readily evident to an audience (at least not to me).

Native New Yorkers, Bernard born in 1930, Tavel in 1941, and Ludlam in 1943, all three are city sophisticates of considerable education. Ludlam has a B.A. in dramatic art, Tavel an M.A. in philosophy and literature, and Bernard a Ph.D. in language and literature. Ludlam and Tavel are given to long academic disquisitions about a style that critic Bonnie Marranca designates as 'sexual exuberance and transvestism, the mix-and-match of 'high' and 'low' culture, camp, visual flamboyance, and comic humiliation of respectable figures.' The Ridiculous is a far cry from the surface realism of Duberman or Patrick.

Of the three, Ludlam alone has received the accolades of a *New Yorker* profile and the unstinting admiration of Stefan Brecht. Ludlam's signal achievement has been to hold together – sometimes with glue and Scotch tape – a theatre company dedicated to staging his plays. About half of his dozen plays have been published, mainly in periodicals. His plays are nineteenth-century in spirit – vehicles for the actor-manager-star – and late twentieth-century in free-swinging burlesque, obscenity, sexuality. Gradually, Ludlam has learned to construct plots and even to sustain characters. By his own account, he moved from the epic (by which he seems to mean the episodic) to the well-made play. *Turds in Hell* (1969, in collaboration with actor Bill Vehr) represents the first technique, and the more popular

125

Bluebeard (1970) the second.

The infernal episodes of *Turds in Hell* are played for sexual exuberance rather than intelligible sequence. Turzahnelle abandons her newborn son Orgone on a mountain-top where he is found by Carla. A large cast of infernal sinners is gathered by Baron Bubbles, a Brazilian Brassiere Buster, who shits money. Romances ensue between the Baron and Turzahnelle, Orgone and nun Vera (Orgone: 'I'm trisexual. I'll try anything.') A St Obnoxious is martyred, and the Baron kidnaps Carla who longs for Orgone. Unknown to one another, Turzahnelle and Orgone are ferried by Charon, but a shipwreck deposits them on a cannibal island where the Baron is chief cook. Turzahnelle exclaims: 'My cook is goosed', as the cook gooses her. Seated on a toilet-throne, she reviews a parade of flagellants climaxed by a radiant Vera: 'Choirs of angels sing joyously as the curtain falls.' My summary is more linear than the actual performance with its song, dance, parades, slapstick, quick changes of scene and costume, and improvisation so free that performance-time varied between three and four hours.

Beginning with *Bluebeard*, however, the Ridiculous Theatrical Company inserted its typical pansexual *lazzi* (tricks) into a more coherent plot. A combination of Gothic novel, science fiction, and heroic tragedy, *Bluebeard* offered its writer the title role. Bluebeard marries and destroys women, but he does so in the cause of science: 'If only there were some new and gentle genital that would combine with me, and mutually interpenetrated, steer me through this storm in paradise!' Among his con-genital failures is Lamia the Leopard-Woman (originally played by transvestite Mario Montez) and Maggot, his slave. The play opens as the good ship *Lady Vain* deposits Bluebeard's innocent victim, Sybil, who is accompanied by her fiancé Rodney Parker and her Malaprop-spouting governess. Avid for guinea pigs, Bluebeard marries both the women. After successful surgery that grafts a chicken-claw genital on Sybil, who proves to be the daughter of Maggot, the visitors depart. Bluebeard is left to the tender ministrations of Lamia and Sheemish, determined to raise him from mediocrity: 'Come', they parody the Wilbur translation of *The Misanthrope*, 'let us do the best we can to change the opinion of this unhappy man.' The cast has done its best to change attitudes and subvert prejudices about 'normal' sex. Company member Lola Pashalinski has pointed out: 'We're really clean minds in clean bodies . . . . We're making fun of sex.' Some may doubt her first sentence, but not the second.

The Ridiculous Theatrical Company's main vehicle for fun has been burlesque – of the film *Grand Hotel* in *Big Hotel* (1967), of Marlowe's *Tamburlaine* in *When Queens Collide* (1968), of Christian epics in *Whores of Babylon* (1968) and *Turds of Hell* (1969), of H. G. Wells's novel in *Bluebeard* (1970), of the Hatfield–McCoy feud in *Corn* (1972), of television police serials in *Hot Ice* (1974). Ludlam's most popular piece has been *Camille* (1973) with few textual changes from Dumas *fils*. Despite large chunks of undigested *Hamlet*, however, *Stage Blood* (1975) mutes burlesque and transexuality. In Stefan Brecht's description it is 'a not altogether ridiculous because somewhat sincere *Hamlet*, dedicated to the insincerity of the actor and to the love homosexual sons bear their ridiculous fathers.' This seems to me to impose seriousness on a touring production of *Hamlet*, as viewed from the (un)dressing-rooms. A local girl Ophelia is rehearsed by Ludlam–Hamlet, whose Stage Manager–lover is also a playwright. When Ludlam's father, the Actor-Manager–Ghost is murdered, his wife-Gertrude wants her practical-joker–lover–Claudius to rule the company. After a series of melodramatic reversals, the Ghost returns to life, reclaims Ophelia as his mistress, promotes his wife's lover, accepts his son's lover's play for production, and orders more stage blood.

Ludlam himself ordered more stage blood for his parody of Wagner, *Der Ring Gott Farblonjet* (1978), but he has since moved on to other forms of theatre – *Aphrodisimania* for Paul Taylor's Dance Company and cabaret acts for his ventriloquist's dummy Walter Ego. In revivals of *Camille, Bluebeard*, and *Stage Blood*, transexuality and burlesque seem shopworn, but Ludlam's enthusiasm remains fresh. In 1978 he told Gautam Das Gupta of *Performing Arts Journal*:

> Gay people have always found a refuge in the arts, and the Ridiculous theatre is notable for admitting it. The people in it – and it is a very sophisticated theatre, culturally – never dream of hiding anything about themselves that they feel is honest and true and the best part of themselves. NOTHING is concealed in the Ridiculous.

Ludlam might be describing the whole genre rather than his own company, and the first theoretician of that genre is Ronald Tavel. As early as Spring 1966, Tavel wrote in *TriQuarterly*: ' . . . what I wanted was the flat and uncagey irrevocability of "ridiculous" . . . . Theatre of the Ridiculous is a community of Ourselves taking momentary time to laugh at its position as the ridiculous.' He names the main influences as Pop, Camp, Psychodelic, and Art Nouveau, but he does not mention the homosexual ambience. The most prolific of the Ridiculous playwrights, Ronald Tavel, has written about two dozen plays as well as a novel, essays, films, and verse. He distinguishes early from later (post-

Gorilla Queen) plays: 'In the early plays I . . . attempted to destroy plot and character, motivation, cause, event, and logic along with their supposed consequences. The word was all. . . . The full-length plays after *Gorilla Queen* obey, I believe *[*Aristotle's*]* difficult insights.' Although Tavel wrote plays when he was still in his teens, he gained notoriety through his film scenarios for Andy Warhol (1964–6). Because Warhol rejected Tavel's *Shower* (1965), it was staged live by John Vaccaro. And thus the Play-house of the Ridiculous was born. This firstborn already bears the family features – disjointed episodes rather than plot, shifting identities of characters, burlesque of and affection for popular genres, obscene word play, hints of Pirandellianism or play within the play. *Shower* still fascinates Tavel, who described it as 'action-packed and streamlined for movement, yet totally devoid of character or identity, direction, plot, or subject matter'. Actually, plot and burlesque characters are susceptible to summary but are scarcely worth it.

During the next two years Tavel wrote other short plays in swift succession – *Vinyl, Kitchenette, The Life of Juanita Castro,* and *The Life of Lady Godiva,* which were not produced in the order written. *Lady Godiva* is perhaps the most popular of this group. Originally played by a man, the lady rides on an elongated horse equipped with steering-wheel, rear-view mirror, brake, gas-pedal; this contraption is driven by Peeping Tom (played by Charles Ludlam). The lady seeks new soles in Coventry Convent, where a corps of transvestite nuns are ruled by Mother Superviva (played by Vaccaro): 'Nudity is the quintessence of essence, though it is sickrilegious to say so.' After sexual fun and games, 'Lady Godiva rides nude at high noon' on Mother Super-viva, but Sister Kasha Veronicas cobbles the soles and shoes the naked lady.

Tavel produced a few plays in order to fill out an evening in the theatre. When *Shower* lasted only an hour, Tavel composed *The Life of Juanita Castro,* which 'should never be rehearsed' since its form is a rehearsal – for a film. (It was filmed by Warhol.) The director and Juanita are played by men, while Fidel, Raul, and Che are played by women. Except for a revolutionary monologue by Fidel and an anti-revolutionary song by Juanita, the director speaks all the lines – scenic directions *and* dialogue for the actors, who are thus manipulated by the director as the politicians' peoples are manipulated. Tavel has claimed that this play is a protest against political manipulation of the artist, but it is hard to hear this through his transexual characters.

Indira Gandhi's Daring Device (1966), a 'smellodrama', was again too short for a full evening, so Tavel wrote *Screen Test* which soon usurped most of the evening because of actor Ludlam's irrepressible improvisations. As in *Juanita Castro,* a director rehearses for a film; his two actresses are a transvestite (originally played by Mario Montez, who himself burlesqued 1940s actress Maria Montez) and a mere woman. In performance the woman did not attain the panache of the transvestite, who perfectly rendered feminine sexuality as synthesized by Hollywood. A second transvestite then competed with the first – actor Charles Ludlam as Norma Desmond, an aging Hollywood star aching for a comeback, who is instead kidnapped by a gorilla.

In 1967 the gorilla-actor, Harvey Tavel, became the director of his brother's *Kitchenette,* which burlesques domestic comedy through a film rehearsal. In a littered kitchenette (replete with improbable toilet) Harvey Tavel directed two couples, female Jo and male Mikie, male Joe and female Mickey: 'Well, why the hell does everybody around here have to have the same name? How am I supposed to know who to have sex with?' Stabbing in the dark, they soon resort to violence. After cross-couplings, Jo stabs Mikie with a marshmallow fork and is in turn strangled on a mattress, as the remaining three actors intone: 'Matric-ide on a mattress!'

Moving to longer plays, Tavel wrote *Gorilla Queen* (1967) which he sees as the first of his Aristotelian dramas. Enlarging the role of the gorilla of *Screen Test,* this ambitious play became the occasion of Tavel's declaration of independence from director John Vaccaro, who demanded abridgements. Tavel moved it intact to the Judson Memorial Church, where it was directed by Living Theatre veteran Lawrence Kornfeld. Set in a Hollywood jungle, *Gorilla Queen* casts transexual Queen Kong as the object of Clyde Batty's quest. Tavel considers his play to have a linear Aristotelian plot, but it is hard to extract beginning, middle, and end from these movie scenes in a mix-master, where a White Woman and Sister Carries are played by men. Clyde shoots Kong and somehow becomes him/her through a Deus Sex Mattachine. Most un-Aristotelian is the shotgun-wedding finale: 'I pronounce you man and wife, or man and man, or ape and man, or queen and woman, or queen and man, or queen and queen, or ape and ape up and up.'

In his next few plays Tavel caricatures contemporary America less affectionately. *Arenas of Lutetia* (1968) combines Greek and Christian myths in two brothers Actaeon and Sebastian. The latter is the author of *Arenas of Lutetia* – the Pirantavel twist – and the arenas are a jungle of creation presided over by muse Lutetia in a *lingua franca* of sexual puns that mock Bohemian America and Hollywood epics. Inhabitually economical is Tavel's next play, which is sometimes considered his best. *Boy on the Straight-Back Chair* (1969) is frighteningly heterosexual (as

131

implied in the title's 'straight') in dramatizing 'our town's dirty laundry' or seduction-murders by Toby Short. Based on actual murders committed by Charles Schmid, the play also draws upon other 'pleasure' killers in our violent society. Subduing his invention, Travel renounces the ridiculous in this grim drama of the humourless playboy of the American West.

After several contemporary satires, Tavel produced his favourite play *Bigfoot* (1970). Unpublished, the play's title refers to the Abominable Snowman, and the play itself stuffs a Pirantavel frame with the old Romantic theme of divided brothers – Esau and Jacob (who becomes Jack), Alpha and Omega, and, finally, Ronald Tavel's actual brother Harvey who arranges Jack's departure through the audience. Having scorned the intellect in essay and burlesque, Tavel surprisingly wrote this turgid debate rather than drama, with long metaphysical speeches supplanting action.

In *Queen of Greece* (1973, also unpublished) he attempts to embed his old Ridiculous techniques in a Platonic dialogue à la *Bigfoot*. Not only Platonic dialogue but also the man Plato himself – as drag queen. The titular queen, however, is Jackie, married to Aristotle, and avid for a crown in the dictatorship of Papapiguous. Originally entitled *How Jacqueline Kennedy Became Queen of Greece,* the play mercilessly caricatures Aristotle Onassis and his wife Jackie, a C.I.A. agent Sam, radical Melina, dictator Papapiguous, and lady's man Andreas/Byron/Jack. Act I ends when Plato stabs Andreas in the back with Jackie's scissors. In Act II Socrates in his cell awaits the historical hemlock. After Alcibiades grieves for his lover's death, Jackie and Melina exchange catty insults. Socrates refuses the dictator's bribes and remarks without grandiloquence: 'I die for democracy against my better judgment.' Just before Socrates drinks the hemlock (from a bedpan), Alcibiades loses his temper and uses a word that recalls Tavel's earlier work: 'I wish your killings pomped with less circumstances than Socrates' has been. This judging and proposing bench's lightning proposals have reduced his death to the *ridiculous*!' (my emphasis). Dying as in David's painting, Socrates dissolves to Kennedy being assassinated. Jackie emerges from the bloody limousine and babbles disconnectedly to the audience. Suddenly sensitive and victimized, she is dragged up a flight of steps and crowned as queen of Greece. The last scene is a curious coda that counters the burlesque body of the play, in which homosexuality wears two contrasting masks, the affectionate devotion of Socrates and Alcibiades, the power-thirst of drag queen Plato.

Although Tavel continues to write (but not to be published) – the anti-colonial *Last Days of British Honduras* (1974), *Gazelle-Boy* (1977), *The Ark of God* (1978), *The Nutcracker in The Land of Nuts* (1979) – it suits my purpose to summarize his *Ovens of Anita Orangejuice: A History of Modern Florida* (revised 1978). Based on the career of Anita Bryant, the play traces her evangelistic struggle for the repeal of the gay rights amendment. Although Tavel clearly disapproves of her talk of 'homowreckuality' and 'homoineffectuals', he does not caricature her crudely. Or rather, he gradually enlarges her from caricature to character – with inconsistent brush-strokes. Mack Hack cynically supports her; his wife Truth Hack clumsily opposes her. Shoily Spellingbee and Alvin Darkperson gain materially from her crusade, but Anita herself is disinterested: 'Kill a Queer for Christ.' Tavel curbs his verbal pyrotechnics, but he does indulge in burlesquing stock types in a huge cast. Only a Cuban refugee, Los Olvidados, is an entirely sympathetic homosexual – who is lynched in the torrent of hatred undiked by Anita. Much of Anita's power rests on telephone calls to specific individuals – powerful or gullible; during the course of the play telephone booths become imprisoning boxes, which in turn become crematoria – the titular ovens of Anita Orangejuice. Having effected a holocaust, Anita ends alone on stage, as far as possible from a ringing telephone, and she closes the play: 'Who is calling?' Tied to her telephone, she has no understanding of communication. It is a curiously sympathetic ending for one who has fanned a holocaust. In actual fact, the Florida Citrus Commission terminated Anita Bryant's contract after twelve years; it would be wishful thinking to credit Tavel for that.

Tavel's transexual exuberance and linguistic games are muted in his plays of the 1970s. The uncommitted ridicule of the earlier plays seems definitively behind him, displaced by linear but clumsy plots and ponderous undramatic monologues. A man of learning, he may be backing away from the stage and into the study.

Of the three Ridiculous playwrights, Kenneth Bernard is personally self-effacing. A family man with an academic position, he has written the most outrageous plays of all, and is very much aware of it:

> I like to think of my plays as metaphors, closer to poetic technique (the coherence of dream) than to rational discourse. I am not interested in traditional plot or character development . . . I would hope the appeal of my plays is initially to the emotions only, not the head, and that they are received as spectacle and a kind of gorgeous (albeit frightening) entertainment. The characters in my plays can often be played by either men or women.

134

In John Vaccaro's direction, the protagonists were sometimes played by transvestites, sometimes by hermaphrodites, sometimes doubled as men and women. In contrast to Ludlam's grotesque sex on stage, to Tavel's transexual panache, the sexual ambiguity in Bernard's plays is at once magnetic and minatory.

Bernard's first produced play *The Moke-Eater* (1968) initiated the Bernard–Vaccaro partnership that has lasted over a decade. Bernard's plays are written with a sure and steady hand, not subject to improvisation and not readily amenable to directorial tampering. Vaccaro was captivated by *The Moke-Eater* at the very time that Ludlam and his actors left the Play-house of the Ridiculous. He arranged its production in a restaurant, since greedy and grotesque eating is a repetitive activity in the play. Exposing 'our town's dirty laundry' differently from Tavel, *The Moke-Eater* still preserves plot and character. A contemporary Willy Loman drives into a small town to have his car repaired. The mechanic calls him Fred although he claims to be Jack, and, faced with moronic mumbling of a crowd, he resorts to pidgin English: 'Car no good. Car go click-click. Car bad. Me want fix car. Me pay. *(He waves the money.)* You understandee 'melican boy? Chop-chop?' As the villagers repeat 'Click-click', a dapper leader emerges from their midst: 'Hello, there. I'm Alec. *(He pauses.)* Smart* Alec.' And smart he proves to be – much smarter than Jack, whom he subjects to a series of humiliations as his only way to escape from the town's stranglehold. Jack is forced to play an animated cartoon, Amos and Andy, an appreciator of the American landscape, a song-and-dance man, a formal dinner guest; he is subjected to sexual titillation. Starved while others gorge themselves, tantalized sexually and politically with a promise of release, prevented even from urinating, Jack is finally

135

reduced to inchoate crying before 'an amorphous form' – the moke-eater – devours an old man. Only then is Jack allowed to get into his repaired car and leave. But three hours later he re-enters the town, with everyone frozen in their positions of the play's opening. It takes a moment before Jack realizes his situation: 'I left here, I tell you. I left here. *(Shouting)* I tell you I left here!' Only in production did *The Moke-Eater* show the marks of the Ridiculous – in transexual adornments of furs and feathers, in occasional sallies of demonic laughter, in a female Alec who directs the victimization of Jack for his and our delectation.

Bubi, the Master of Ceremonies in Bernard's next play, his often-performed *Night Club* (1970), is 'strikingly made up as a woman, but dressed in a tuxedo'. Although his/her sex is indeterminate, the sexuality is 'clear and strong'. In Vaccaro's production the role was doubly played by a veteran Ridiculous actress, Mary Waranow, and a well-known transvestite Ondine, both of whom were infused with Vaccaro's own demonic, often sadistic energy. The titular night club is Bubi's Hide-Away, where the performers are drawn from an onstage audience who chant Bubi's name as though he were a saviour. And he may be, given the mysterious threatening sounds from the world beyond the night club. Only Bubi and the transvestite light-man can organize entertainment in this garish asylum. Bubi is a cruel master, demanding humiliations like his predecessor Alec, and finally he inveigles the cast to its own 'paradise now' in mass copulation – to the theme music of the Lone Ranger. The one resister is guillotined, and Bubi sets his head on a table. *Night Club* closes as Bubi repeats his escapist song, resonant with the horrifying routines it has called forth. The severed head croaks Bubi's name repeatedly, until he is drowned out by bulldozers and jackhammers, which are in turn drowned out by the sound of wings flapping high in the sky.

The Magic Show of Dr Ma-Gico (1973) adheres to the same format of master of ceremonies governing perform-ance numbers: 'I do *not* deal in tricks . . . . I deal in life . . . . True magic is metaphor.' Instead of the night-club back-ground, the play is set in a seventeenth-century aristocratic drawing room backed by mirrors, with throne at the centre, and audience on three sides. Each of the numbers climaxes in violence – a clumsy king knifed in the belly, a young commoner hanged, Esmeralda smothered by gypsies, a young lover castrated during fellatio, a prince killing a king by error, a queen literally loved to death, and, after knave, courtier, and nobleman fail to kill a king, Dr Ma-Gico himself slits his throat. Elegant dances punctuate the numbers in the demonic magic show.

The Sixty-Minute Queer Show (1977, as yet unpublished) joins Ma-Gico's powerless kings to the drag queens of the Ridiculous. Although Bernard has written (in a letter to me) that *The Sixty-Minute Queer Show* is 'not particularly about queers', he nevertheless highlights homosexuality by punctuating his vaudeville turns with drag queens – no less than ten in his script but reduced to three in Vaccaro's production. Become a composite portrait, the Drag Queen, that most ostentatious of queers, parallels the director-figure of Bernard's earlier plays. Hard-edged, double-sexed, prismatic, the Drag Queen manipulates his/her audience as the director manipulates his actors, and he/she does so with skill and style – literally a variety show. In *The Sixty-Minute Queer Show* the drag queens of the interludes are distorted echoes of nominal queens within the scenes, who inevitably oppose the kings. Two recurrent Bernard types blend in *The Sixty-Minute Queer Show* – ruling figures of a political world and artist figures of an aesthetic world, perhaps mutually exclusive.

The eight scenes dramatize rehearsals of various tortures of characters who are vaguely familiar from legend and literature – king and commoner, lascivious queen and Don Juan lover, trial of a king, circus performers, Cleopatra abandoned by her cowboy lover, a ballet scene, a parade of dancers. Although the scenes are more fragmentary and disjunctive than ever before in Bernard's work, a picaresque plot finally emerges, with the King an inverted *picaro*. In Scene 1 the King 'stuffs Marie with food at all her openings', resulting in his sexual climax and her death. After the last scene in the final Drag Queen number, an intermittent spotlight plays 'on the King's body, otherwise unseen, with its bleeding slit throat'. Between violent death and violent death, the King evolves from victimizer to victim. He seems to be the heterosexual *par excellence*, while homosexuals enter several scenes – the farmer's son wants to be a hairdresser, and his sister needs a shave; Cleopatra is a gross black male; the whole cast perform ballet steps like the ballet-dancers de Trocadero – and the image of the Drag Queen hovers over the whole.

One often hears the cliché that reality is so theatrical that theatre pales in comparison. Bernard theatricalizes its obverse: theatre (especially popular theatre) is so sadistically theatrical that reality pales by comparison. A Drag Queen intones: 'Queer is queerer than you think . . . . Throw a fish to a queer tomorrow.' In so doing, we make of him/her a *queer fish,* or anyone who dares to deviate from the norm. Stefan Brecht's comment is apposite: 'The scenes present the norm, an idiotic, sadistic humanity, their story the again and again delayed imminent then achieved slitting (at the queen's instigation) of the weakly vicious (heterosexual) king's throat.' The slitting is also art, a theatre of cruelty without catharsis.

Queer queen as word play, actor's play, and symbolic play functions for Bernard as a multi-faceted metaphor. It subsumes earlier dramatist's pleas for sexual freedom or sexual tolerance, their landscapes of the homosexual jungle, Camp burlesques of classics and commercials, transexual mockery of heterosexual sex stars, Bernard's own sadistic manipulation of sex as torture. Central to his drama is the transexual role of artist/master of magic or ceremonies. Far from catharsis, he/she theatrically arouses fear and desire, slaking them only slightly as the show stampedes on.

Gay theatre usually leans to light surfaces. Under them Duberman and Patrick plead for sexual tolerance. Under them Ludlam and Tavel begin by burlesquing our sexist society and its reflexion in sexist art. At about the same time – the end of the 1960s – these two playwrights moved from merry pansexual Bedlams toward more linear plots involving more coherent characters, with Tavel reaching for a philosophic message. In contrast, successive Bernard plays increasingly decimate plot and character to theatricalize sadistic moments, extremist climaxes toward which his homosexuals act as director/catalysts. Through Bernard's metaphoric queers, the Ridiculous theatre resembles Artaud's Theatre of Cruelty. With curious prescience, Albee's intermittently cruel Martha announced this grave gay theatre: 'I have a fine sense of the ridiculous but no sense of humor.'

8
Verbals:
Lowell, McClure, Owens

'Verbals' is an odd title for a chapter in a book that predicates its subject matter upon the verbal primacy of performance material, but I select it to underline the contrast with my next chapter, 'Visuals'. In contrast to the 1950s, the period between 1960 and 1980 was deeply suspicious of words, and few poets were attracted to theatre. In the 1950s the Beat poets offered their readings as theatrical events – especially Duncan, Ginsberg, Snyder – whereas the plays of such poets as Eberhart, Jeffers, Nemerov, Schevill, Williams were often less dramatic than their lyrics.

Robert Lowell (1917–77), however, that superlative and 'heartbreaking' poet (his own preferred adjective) wrote three memorable plays, after translating Racine and Aeschylus to limber up his dramatic sense. *The Old Glory* traces American history through stories of Hawthorne and Melville. The two Hawthorne-based plays are set in colonial times, but for Lowell the seed of imperial United States is sown in seventeenth-century Puritan Massachusetts and in eighteenth-century Boston. The Melville-based play foreshadows the Civil War and contemporary racial conflict; it has been most popular on the stage, often played alone. Conceived as a whole, the three plays are entitled *The Old Glory,* but far from celebrating the flag, they dramatize the consistency of American commerce and violence.

Endecott and the Red Cross (revised in 1969), the first play of the trilogy, takes subject and title from Hawthorne, but Lowell also uses another Hawthorne story about Endecott, 'The Maypole of Merry Mount', as well as Thomas Morton's *New English Canaan* (1637). Morton becomes the Anglican antagonist to Lowell's Puritan protagonist Endecott. Their competing commercial interests sharpen ideological conflict, which finally erupts into Endecott's rebellion against British rule. Most of the dialogue takes the form of flexible blank verse, broken at tense moments.

Lowell's Endecott can remember his courtly youth, before the death of his wife turned him into a soldier needing a stern religion. He is still prey to gentle memories, so that he countermands the punitive dicta of Elder Palfrey, who is invented by Lowell. Yet Endecott narrates his dream in which he *is* Elder Palfrey, preacher and executioner, committing cruelties in the name of a rigid religion. By the end of Lowell's play, Endecott acts out the dream; opposing the king's rule in the person of Morton, he addresses his soldiers in words that he himself describes as 'half truth, half bombast'. In cutting the Red Cross flag of England from its staff, Endecott takes the first violent step that will result in the supremacy of Old Glory.

The second play of Lowell's trilogy, *My Kinsman, Major Molineux* (1964) based on Hawthorne's story of that name, takes place a century and a half later, on the eve of the

American Revolution, and Lowell conveys the feverish climate in a shorter verse line of loose tetrameters, sometimes rhymed. The protagonist, eighteen-year-old Robin, comes to Boston to seek his fortune, hoping for favour from his kinsman, Major Molineux, the British governor. Within the day that Robin spends in the city, his country innocence crumbles into complicity in the lynching of his kinsman. Lowell invents a younger brother for Robin, who is at once more innocent and more self-absorbed during their long city day that initiates them into corruption and rebellion. In the last scene Robin and his brother see their kinsman Major Molineux, tarred and feathered by rebels. Even while pitying his kinsman, Robin 'unconsciously' waves the rebel Rattlesnake flag in his face, and his brother 'unthinkingly' offers dirt to be flung at the Loyalist Major. When the crowd have killed the Major, they cheer the Republic. Alone, the two brothers repeat that Major Molineux is dead. Tainted with that death, neither of them mentions that the Major was their kindly kinsman. Again the flag was a rallying-point for man's inhumanity to man.

In *Benito Cereno* (1964) Lowell follows the events of the Melville novella – in lush blank verse – only to subvert its intention. In this third play, we actually see Old Glory, the standard of Yankee Captain Delano's ship, *President Adams*. Lowell's play opens with a 'machinelike' salute to the American flag, which is implicitly challenged by the pirate flag on the slave-ship *San Domingo* – a black skull and crossbones on white ground. Slavery as piracy is a metaphor of accretive meaning in Lowell's play, set on American Independence Day. Captain Delano states the American position: 'Everyone disbelieves in slavery and wants slaves.'

When Lowell's Captain Delano boards the *San Domingo*

captained by Don Benito Cereno, he disapproves of the dirt and lack of discipline. Once aboard, Delano is almost hypnotized by the heat and buzzing insects, by the rambling of Captain Cereno and the unction of his slaves. Patronizing and friendly to Spanish Benito Cereno, Delano is patronizing and superior to the Negro Babu. While Don Benito is taking his siesta, Babu 'entertains' Captain Delano with four spectacles that subtly comment on the cruel complexity of racial relations. Later Delano is a spectator at grotesque scenes – an African king festooned with chains, Babu shaving Cereno with the Spanish flag as towel, a formal dinner with 'La Marseillaise' as background music. When Delano's (invented) boatswain Perkins warns the Captain that the Negroes have taken command of the slave ship, the Yankee is incredulous. He watches disapprovingly as Don Benito walks across the Spanish flag to kiss a skull, and when his boatswain takes the same path. When his own turn comes, Delano points his gun at Babu. Fortunately for him, American aid arrives, and Babu raises a white handkerchief, calling: 'The future is with us.' 'This is your future', retorts Delano and shoots Babu dead. In contrast to Melville's Delano, a man of good will with limited perceptions, Lowell's Delano is a man whose good will is eroded by his limited perceptions. Behind Delano's smoking gun, Old Glory is immanent.

Gerald Weales has acutely summarized Lowell's trilogy: '*The Old Glory* is about revolution – Endecott initiates one, Robin joins one, Delano puts one down . . . . The movement in time from play to play . . . underlines the basic theme that, under whatever flag, power demands action and the action is inevitably violent and tyrannical.' Guns are ubiquitous as banners on stage, and commerce threads through the dialogue. Dry or rich as needed, Lowell's language is supply suited to the exigencies of each

play – alternatively discursive and abrupt in *Endecott,*
informal for the brothers of *Molyneux* but counterpointed
against the inflammatory slogans of the mob, and in *Benito
Cereno* the laconic Yankee arrogance resonates against
rich Latinisms or exotic Black phrases. Lowell has been
adversely criticized for taking 'a curiously old-fashioned
view of theater as primarily the verbal interaction of actors
advancing the plot', but the selected plots of *Old Glory*
dramatize a synchronic view of America – then pregnant
with now. The verbal interaction of Lowell's characters is
intensified by his mastery of image and rhythm. He has also
been criticized for interpolating dream and spectacle into
drama, but these devices deepen the interactions of
characters even when they do not advance the plot.
Granted nevertheless that Lowell's is a traditional view of
theatre, he executes it with the superb verbal resources of a
heartbreaking poet. It is some measure of the diversity of
American theatre of the 1960s that his plays opened in an
Off-Off-Broadway venue – Wynn Handman's American
Place Theatre and won the Best Play Obie.

Michael McClure is a free-swinging, non-revising poet.
Born in 1932 in Kansas, educated in the midwest and
southwest, he came to San Francisco in 1953 and has lived
there ever since. Like his friends Allen Ginsberg and Gary
Snyder, McClure read his verse aloud, but McClure alone
went from these theatrical readings to theatre. His plays
fall into three quite distinct groups: (1) Early pieces whose
action is static and whose free verse lines tend to swell in
rhetorical bombast; (2) Flights of fantasy peopled by
talking plants, animals, minerals, or asteroids, who are
caught up in small human adventures; (3) Adaptations into
contemporary idiom of classics of our culture. Produced
Off-Off-Broadway and its West Coast counterpart,
McClure's plays have gradually been accommodated in

more profitable locations: *General Gorgeous* (1975) was commissioned for a theatre on San Francisco's Broadway, and *Red Snake* was scheduled for Joe Papp's Public Theatre in 1981.

McClure has declared: 'Theatre is an organism of poetry – weeping and laughing, and crying, and smiling, and performing superhuman acts – on a shelf in space and lit with lights.' Similar vague pronouncements sprinkle the three plays published as *Mammals,* a title that would seem to contradict the 'superhuman' of the quotation, but for McClure everything in the cosmos is related. The theme of *Mammals,* as of McClure's poems and *Meat Science Essays* of the early 1960s, is that human beings forget at their peril that they are animals, mammals, meat. Loudly sensual and anti-intellectual, the Beat poets of the 1950s sang the same tune as the Off-Off-Broadway playwrights of the 1960s, and McClure, who belongs to both groups, phrases his 'meat science' in a mixture of abstraction and obscenity in *The Blossom* (1958), *!The Feast!* (1960), and *The Pillow* (1961).

In his best-known play *The Beard* (1965), McClure first married language to action. A *succès de scandale,* the hour-long mating rite unites archetypal American characters from different eras – Jean Harlow, the 1940s Hollywood sex goddess who died at the age of twenty-six, and Billy the Kid, the late-nineteenth-century outlaw who was shot at twenty-two, and who appeared in McClure's *Blossom.* The pretentious rhetoric of McClure's early plays is assigned to Jean Harlow, now mocked by the animality of the situation; the rough talk that erupted spasmodically in McClure's early plays is assigned to Billy the Kid, who converts it to tenderness. (The contrast is apparent in the title of a volume of poems published after the play – *The Sermons of Jean Harlow and the Curses of Billy the Kid.*)

145

The Beard is structured in a single act of rising tension that climaxes (pun intended) in cunnilingus, but the rise divides into five movements: (1) Billy pursues Harlow with words; (2) Harlow sits on his lap but teases him about his desire; (3) they jockey for supremacy, speaking in explicitly sexual terms, until, about midway through the play, Billy bites Harlow's foot; (4) although they continue to duel verbally, the action becomes more erotic; (5) Harlow is frustrated by mere words but admits: 'You're insane and violent but I like you!' Throughout the play Harlow has repeated her opening line obsessively: 'Before you can pry any secrets from me, you must first find the real me!' By the play's end, Billy appropriates the line, and the two join in the sexual embrace that defines 'the real me' of both.

Extravagant claims have been made for the play, as in Norman Mailer's introduction of 'ghosts from two periods of the American past . . . at the same time . . . present in our living room undressing themselves or speaking to us of the nature of seduction, the nature of attraction, and particularly, the nature of perverse temper between a man and a woman.' Some of us have different living rooms, but more to the point is the living room that McClure stages, with fur-covered table and chairs under an orange light. Lest we take the mating rite as seriously as Mailer, McClure stipulates that both characters 'wear small beards of torn white tissue paper', whence the title. The play is often revived, redolent of the innocent 1960s when a declaration of independent vocabulary was confused with independence, and sexual freedom with freedom. *The Beard* is something of an anomaly in McClure's writing, since the characters are historical, behaving at once like myths and animals. The inhabitual prose dialogue – sermons and curses – is effortlessly funny.

Most of McClure's plays, however, are fantasies striving

to present a world of flora, fauna, and nudes who are at one with the universe, 'since everything is everything anyway'. Eleven short scenes collected in *Gargoyle Cartoons* (1971) are more cartoon than gargoyle. The characters are flower people, talking Pandas, killer moths, a spider rabbit, pig people replaced by mouse people, silver ducklings, a snoutburbler, a Pyramid, Square, Cylinder, Cube, a talking Bed, a Jesus Voice, and a Camus Voice. Intended for performance in random mix-and-matches, the sketches are frail. Appreciation of this major phase of McClure's drama turns upon which suffix one adds to the word 'child'. For the appreciators, among whom is the director John Lion, these inventive sketches have a child*like* charm; for detractors, the ubiquitous triviality seems child*ish*. (I also find the plays of poet Kenneth Koch, which I have never seen performed, too child*ish* to examine in a book intended for adults.)

Having tossed off the eleven *Gargoyle Cartoons,* McClure went on to full-length fantasies – *The Cherub* (1970), *Grabbing the Fairy* (1973), *Gorf* (1974), *Minnie Mouse Meets the Tap-Dancing Buddha* (1975), *General Gorgeous* (1975), *The Masked Choir* (1976), and a host of others. The titles are usually an index to the particular animal–human or fantasy event, although it would be hard to guess that *Gorf* is a flying phallus with prodigious powers.

After the Bicentennial year, 1976, McClure somewhat abruptly entered his third phase – adaptation of classics. It is evident why Kafka's *Mouse-Singer* would attract this 'meat science' poet, and in adapting it to his *Josephine the Mouse-Singer,* McClure stages human mice in varieties of Victorian costume. A Narrator follows closely Kafka's text, although McClure breaks Kafka's clauses into free verse lines. Narration soon gives way to dramatic scenes of

147

the brief childhood of Josephine, the judges' refusal to exempt her from labour in order to give herself to art, Josephine's quarrel with sycophants, her rejection of an un-Kafkan suitor named Baby, the hovering of mouse–ghosts including the suitor who killed himself for unrequited love of Josephine. McClure's Josephine expounds a romantic view of the universality of her art, for which she takes a vow of celibacy. Toward the end of McClure's play the Narrator quotes Kafka's last few sentences on the disappearance of the singer but the durability of her legend. McClure, however, brings Josephine back to sing ecstatically while the suicides dance around her. Only then does McClure's Narrator end formally: 'Thus our drama ends–/ bringing myth and truth/ to watchers and to friends.' With relative simplicity, McClure has subdued his toy animals to the exigencies of Kafka's ambiguous bestiary.

Unlike *Josephine, Goethe: Ein Fragment* (1978) is not a full-fledged adaptation but a fragmentary fantasy around Goethe's *Faust*. McClure's play opens with a fully clothed Goethe in bed with a nude woman. When she leaves, Goethe asks: 'If this were a play would/ it perform? My life is a series/ of fragmented secrets/ acted upon/ the open stage.' He answers his question with a McClurian credo: 'Yes, we are the real/ *fragments* of the ghostly/ Universe.' The next scene takes place in a Grecian garden where Mephistopheles introduces himself, offering to immortalize Goethe and allow him an alternative life, if he himself is given a part in the play still to be written. The third scene shifts to two guillotine-makers, casually professional about the instrument that will victimize Gretchen. McClure next has Goethe stab Mephistopheles again and again, but of course Mephistopheles does not die and predicts that he will be the star of *Faust*. The next scene retains the Faust–Gretchen seduction, with Goethe in the role of

Faust, but in the alternative life offered by Mephistopheles, Goethe woos Helen. Mephistopheles worries about the shape of what he regards as *his* play. Gretchen shoots Mephistopheles again and again, but again he does not die. When Gretchen tries to shoot Helen, the pistol is empty. Trying to choose between Gretchen and Helen, Goethe goes mad, and Mephistopheles invites both ladies to lunch. In the final scene Goethe is back in the bed of the opening scene, his dream vivid in his mind. With a large quill-pen he begins to write, and all the other characters come on stage for a final song and dance, but the play's last words are the actual last words of Goethe: 'More light.' McClure should ponder them.

McClure's purpose is not clear to me in his translation of James Shirley's 1641 *Cardinal* to his *Red Snake* (1979, not yet published). Although his programme note affirms: '*The Red Snake* is a serious play', his cross-couplings and ubiquitous obscenities sound more like burlesque. In Shirley's play the titular cardinal is a Byzantine villain, engineering marriage and murder before he dies a suicide. McClure adds sex and violence to the labyrinthine intrigue, clothing his handsome young philanderers in white in Act I, black in Act II. The (prose) dialogue returns to first-wave McClure with splicing of abstraction and obscenity. Because of the flat language, the intended grandeur is poverty-stricken. In an interview McClure affirmed his view of the play as affirmation: 'I'm never hopeless about being a mammal in an ecstatic, living, breathing universe.'

Neither, for that matter, is Rochelle Owens, but of late she seems to be retreating from theatre to her free and energetic lyrics. Born in New York City in 1936, she has worked in art galleries and publishing firms. So strong and sensual are her poems that their author was 'naturally' assumed to be a man. The stridency carries over to her drama. 'Authentic theatre', she has written, 'is always oscillating between joyousness and fiendishness.' So rapid is this oscillation in her plays that it seems simultaneous.

Her first play *Futz* (1959, but revised in 1968) is the most sensational example. Farmer Cyrus Futz mates with his pig Amanda, so joyously that his townsmen find it fiendish: 'And how many tits does your wife have? Mine has twelve.' Majorie Satz reluctantly consents to a three-way orgy. When Oscar Loop and Ann Fox witness the orgy, he kills her and is condemned to hang, fulfilling the loop of his name. Accused of being 'the satan here in our village, Futz is sent to jail where Majorie's brother stabs him. The play is an anti-Puritan parable that suited the mood of Off-Off-Broadway in the 1960s, and was subsequently filmed by the same irreverent director, Tom O'Horgan.

Shifting from an imaginary town to an imaginary Greenland, Owens wrote *The String Game* (1963). The play is named after a game played by gentle Eskimos during their long winter. To the disapproval of their Maltese priest, they associate their string designs with sexual fantasies. Cecil, half-Eskimo and half-German, resents the natives' indifference to his commercial ambition, and he buys the priest's support with spaghetti in rich sauce. Shocked at the priest's gluttony, Cecil slaps him on the back and causes his death by choking. The saddened Eskimos return to their erotic string game.

In *Istamboul* (1965) Owens grounds fantastic history in fantastic geography. During the Crusades, Norman warriors are lured by hirsute Byzantine women, and their wives are attracted to sensual Byzantine men. The clash of cultures mixes joy and ferocity, as St Mary of Egypt murders Norman Godfrigh. His wife Alice and Byzantine Leo make love while waiting for the invasion of the Saracens. Despite its all-embracing title *Homo* (1965),

Owens's next play again dramatizes a culture conflict – between a fantastic West and a fantastic East in the mid-nineteenth century, that time of imperialism. A quotation from Arnold Toynbee precedes the play: 'The most popular of the racial theories of western civilization is that which sets upon a pedestal the xanthotrichous, glaucopian, dolichocephalic variety of homo leucodermaticus, called by some the Nordic man, by Nietzsche "the blond beast".' We do not need the dictionary to suspect that the play will imply: 'Black is beautiful.' Conversely, blond is ugly. Owens takes 'the blond beast' off its pedestal, and she shows its most pernicious representatives to be women. Gelderen, a Dutch trader, accepts any humiliation to make money in the Orient, but his wife teases the workers sexually, and beautiful blond Bernice is a cruel goddess in this mythical land of Oriental wealth.

Homo seems like a first draft of Owens's most savage culture conflict *Beclch* (1966). The fantasy locale shifts to an African village, visited by four white adventurers. One of them, Beclch (with its hints of belch, cluck, kill) becomes a more monstrous goddess than Bernice of *Homo,* not only teasing men erotically, but also torturing and killing by caprice. She sickens her young lover Jose with an initiation into cock-fighting; she inveigles another lover Yago to infect himself with elephantiasis, and then to strangle himself. Her cruelties turn against her, however, since tribal law forbids her to rule without a consort. Vivid and sensual to the last, she savours her own death.

He Wants Shih (1970, but not produced until 1975) again juxtaposes an exotic culture against Western white rationality. After the assassination of his mother, the neophyte Emperor Lan is torn between her political pragmatism and Owens's synthesis of Confucianism and Buddhism. Tempted by scientific rationalism, Lan is saved from it by a kind of rebirth – not from the loins but from the head of his decapitated mother. Only then does he pursue the titular Shih, the feminine part of himself, which is an emblem for Owen's all-embracing mysterious *shur*. Lan reels from adventure to adventure – befriending and then opposing the monk Feng, rejecting the love of a princess for that of his half-brother Bok, withdrawing from both imperialistic Americans and his mother's Chinese rebels. He is imprisoned by Feng for despising the very knowledge he once sought. In the play's final scene Lan-he turns into Lan-she, ecstatically accepting rape by an army: 'Spread out my buttocks! I can be penetrated through by you, all of you!' Unlike Beclch, who is exhilarated by her own lonely death, Lan-she resembles a McClure character in exhilaration at all that is alive and passionate.

Owens's next play, *Kontraption* (1972), tempers such universal acceptance. Abdal and Hortten are, like Emperor Lan, in quest of their essential humanity. When a chemist situates it in the body, Abdal smothers him. Although Hortten permits the murder, he later regrets it. Anti-body Abdal is rewarded with a new form, a square 'with hips and ass'. Delighted with this body, Abdal can offer shelter to Hortten, but the novelty wears off, and he remarks self-depreciatively: 'I am a contraption with shoes!' Only when square Abdal resorts to rape, does he regain his human form. As he again undertakes to 'pierce the mystery of God', he dies in his frailty – perhaps Owens's warning about those who fail to accept their human animality.

Owens's first volume of plays, published in 1968, notes the data of first productions, but such data are given for only one play in her second volume, published in 1974 (containing *He Wants Shih* and *Kontraption*, both subsequently performed). Her large casts, relentlessly strident language, compulsion for the actors to start 'high' – have diminished production possibilities in a theatre of diminishing spectrum, but her admirers are loyal with praise. In 1975 the avant-garde review *Margins* devoted much of an issue to eulogy of her poems and plays, with an enthusiastic overview by Kenneth Bernard. He praises her *Karl Marx Play* (1973) as a humanization of Marx 'at the same time that it maintains the myth'. We see Marx assailed by family problems, by financial worries from which Engels rescues him, and, most inventively, by the scolding of Black singer Leadbelly, who rubs Marx's nose in his entrails: 'Marx has guts – and he lets it all hang out.' But Marx is afflicted with 'Five kinder, a wife and a lousy case of boils.' Upper-class wife Jenny and perennial rebel Leadbelly fight for the possession of the soul of Karl Marx. With no attempt at a chronological story, the play intersperses songs (to Galt MacDermot's music) and long passages of theory of play. Finally, Leadbelly succeeds in energizing Marx: 'He puts a flaming torch to Marx's intestines. The others are dumbfounded as Marx, with a surge of superhuman energy, dashes off – to write *Das Kapital*.' Paradoxically, animal pain spurs Marx to superhuman efforts that transform life for whole populations.

Less well-integrated with energetic animalism is another Owens drama obliquely based on history, *Emma Instigated Me* (1975, but subsequently revised). Emma Goldman offers Owens a scope comparable to that of Marx, but against her is juxtaposed, not the salty colour of Leadbelly, but a Pirandellian Author. Goldman and fictional Author quarrel about the play in progress: 'Nothing connects in this play', Goldman pedantically complains. Although bifurcating into a visible character and a Recorded Voice, the Author wants to follow her own associative bent.

Emma's erotic entanglements alternate with her compassion for exploited women. Like Carol Bolt's *Red Emma,* this one is ambiguous; or rather, Owens creates an ambiguous portrait of a self-indulgent woman who nevertheless feels pity for others; of a dogmatic woman who nevertheless fights for freedom; of a near nymphomaniac who is also an ardent feminist. Owens does not assimilate these contradictions into drama. Self-obsessed, her Emma is less dynamic than her Marx, and her Author is far less pungent than her Leadbelly. Fantastic history can rise to emotional vigour, but probably not through the old conceit about a play-in-progress, *déjá déjà vu* by 1975. Most disappointing – but perhaps this was corrected in the revised version – is the relative flatness of the language, lacking Owens's indomitable energy.

It is nevertheless energy that sizzles through most of Owens's plays, with their spectrum of reactions to the human animal condition. Although she sometimes inclines toward McClure's omnivorous acceptance, her several characters enunciate demurrals, hesitancies, martyrdoms. Rather than characters, however, it is the fantastic landscape that is memorable in a world at once joyous and fiendish. Although McClure sings of this world, which he also examines in adaptations, his bestiary tends to be trivial and domestic. For me at least, Lowell remains the verbal dramatist of highest achievement, gaining painful wisdom.

9
Visuals:
Foreman, Breuer

This chapter hazards the most problematic aspect of contemporary divergent dramaturgy. Librettists do not seem to me playwrights because their words are subservient to music, but some recent drama woos the eye as much as the ear. Six Americans have forged influential visual modes in theatre – Peter Schuman of the Bread and Puppet Theatre, Robert Wilson of the Byrd Hoffman Foundation, Richard Schechner and Spalding Gray of The Performance Group, Richard Foreman of the Ontological/ Hysteric Theatre, and Lee Breuer of the Mabou Mines. All six have published scripts, but the text is only one element of these contemporary avatars of Wagner's *Gesamtkunstwerk* – arts blended in performance. Proportionately, the several texts weigh differently in the several contexts. Schuman's spare, often sung, dialogue rings out of actors hidden behind giant masks of puppets; such dialogue would be dwarfed by mere human delivery. Many of Wilson's scripts evolve from the speech rhythms of an autistic child without whom they are unimaginable (to me). Schechner,

straining toward rituals of *communitas*, constructs environments around adapted classics such as *The Bacchae,
Macbeth, Oedipus, The Balcony*. (Spalding Gray, working
in the same space, has so far published only one of his
autobiographical texts.) These men do not seem to me to be
dramatists, authors of compositions whose main drive is
original words. In contrast, Foreman and Breuer speak of
themselves as playwrights, and both have published collec-
tions of their texts, which are beginning to be performed
outside their particular theatres, with other casts.
Although Breuer and Foreman are steeped in the visual
arts, their plays are rich in words. In confining my
commentary to their words, I am aware of my inadequacy,
for the visual engulfs the verbal in performance, sometimes
drowning it. We are, however, not in performance but in
print.

Richard Foreman was born in New York City in 1937.
While still in high school, he happened upon the works of
Brecht, and was indelibly marked by that playwright's
estrangement effect. After graduating from Brown University, Foreman enrolled for an M.F.A. in John Gassner's
playwriting programme at Yale University, and he still
speaks fondly of that critic, against whose aesthetic he
reacted. But slowly. While still at Yale, Foreman cast
longing eyes toward Broadway, and his plays were tailored
to suit – by his account. Upon receiving his degree,
Foreman moved to New York City where he entered the
playwriting wing of the Actor's Studio. In his own (rather
jaundiced) words about this period: 'One year I imitated
Arthur Miller, the next year Brecht, the next year
Giraudoux.' The only theatre performances that interested
him were those of the Living Theatre, but he was energized
by the underground movies shown in that theatre's building. Foreman found the film-makers' dislocation of time

and space a challenge to his perceptions and a reflection of his own thoughts. He decided to try to stage such dislocations with techniques analogous to those used by Jack Smith, Yvonne Rainer, and, later, Andy Warhol. Filmmaker Jonas Mekas offered Foreman a site – the Cinematheque on Wooster Street. Foreman baptized his theatre even before it was born with the flashy direction-pointer Ontological/Hysteric, which he later described:

> I have always dealt with basically nineteenth-century classic theatrical situations, like boulevard comedy triangles and so forth, and tried to redeem those *[hysterical]* situations by atomizing them, by breaking them apart and letting other considerations bleed through. Those other considerations being, in essence, philosophical, ontological considerations.

Foreman has written over forty plays, directing about two dozen himself but classifying only a dozen as Ontological/ Hysteric Theatre mainly produced between 1975 and 1979 in his own loft with audience confined to seven rows of uncomfortable risers at one end of a long room.

Although Foreman's interviews, essays, and manifestos readily parade his theory, he insists: 'After the fact, I do much theorizing, and *alongside* the fact, I do much theorizing, but things *[performances]* never come from theorizing directly.' Desiring to de-construct traditional (hysterical) drama, Foreman draws his material from a notebook in which he writes continuously. Like Gertrude Stein, whose plays he saw performed at the Judson Memorial Church in the early 1960s, he is obsessed by processes of consciousness and, like her, that is what he seeks to render in his scripts. Foreman has also collaborated with composer Stanley Silverman on musicals and

operas; he has directed a Broadway production of Brecht's
Threepenny Opera; he has made films and videotapes, and
he plans to embark on television work. From 1968 to 1979,
however, he has been devoted to his Ontological/Hysteric
Theatre where he has functioned 'as composer, designer,
writer, director, dance director, you know, everything'.
Protean though he is, Foreman considers that his verbal
text is at the centre of

> a theatre which broke down all elements into a kind of
> atomic structure – and showed those elements of story,
> action, sound, light, composition, gesture, in terms of
> the smallest building-block units, the basic cells of the
> perceived experience of both living and art-making. The
> scripts themselves read like notations of my own process
> of imagining a theatre piece.

The scripts may read that way to their author, who is
re-reading his own thoughts, but they are almost impenetr-
able to the reader who has not experienced them in the
theatre. Although the story-line has often been slighted in
Off-Off-Broadway productions, almost no one jettisons it
as totally as Foreman (after Gertrude Stein). Upon his
Stein base of random associations in the unconscious,
Foreman builds structures influenced by modern French
criticism, which effectively devalues narrative; he calls
them 'decentered structures'. Brecht, Stein, underground
films, and post-structuralist criticism combine in Foreman's art to pulverize plot and emotional characters.
Replacing Aristotelian plot and character with manipulation of space and space-fillers, Foreman is willy-nilly in
Artaud's lineage as well as that of Brecht.

Foreman's texts are tedious to summarize and difficult to
interpret, if one looks for a meaning, as I do, against

Foreman's injunctions. But he desires an audience who will absorb thought through perception:

> I want to refocus the attention of the spectator on the intervals, gaps, relations and rhythms which saturate the objects (acts and physical props) which are the 'givens' of any particular play. In doing this, I believe the spectator is made available (as I am, hopefully, when writing) to those most desirable energies which secretly connect him (through a kind of resonance) with the foundations of his being.

In inviting audience participation, however cool, Foreman joins the main body of divergent contemporary dramatists.

A description of Foreman's plotless Ontological/Hysteric plays would demand this whole book, for they progress from moment to moment, by tableaux rather than incidents; as in film, his continuity consists of frames, and frequent transformations of the visual field recall the jump-cuts of film. His plays sometimes take sonata form: A–B–A or frenzy–almost unbearable slow motion–frenzy. Movement is pervasive, sometimes slight (during the long 'B' section), sometimes tumultuous ('A' and 'C'), each testing the spectator's powers of perception. The reader, as distinguished from the spectator, must imagine manipulation of space and time: *Space* in framing devices through scenic directions about doors, windows, mirrors, or moving planes, and strings that impose attachments while outlining configurations; *Time* in scenic directions about thuds, buzzers, metronomes, raucous music, bare or strobe lights, and masquerading as dialogue, wordless exclamations or meaningless repetitions. Moreover, the printed plays do not indicate when a character speaks 'live' or in Voice-over. On the other hand, the texts *are* in print, and the reader or director is free to betray Foreman's own models of production.

In performance Foreman is always visible at his table, controlling lights, sounds, and the incessant changes of set. Although he rarely leaves that table to manipulate his non-professional actors on stage (like the Polish sculptor–director Tadeusz Kantor), he treats his actors like found objects. Conversely, objects may acquire quasi-human personality – lamps of *Total Recall*, rocks of *Hotel China*, doll-houses of *Sophia III*. 'People are more interesting than props', a Voice-over announces in *Sophia*, but Foreman's plays question the assertion. Occasionally, props may outline gesture, as in two-dimensional painting. Often, Foreman enlarges or dwarfs his props with respect to actors – an aspect of what critic Florence Falk has called his 'aperspectivism'. A text asks mockingly: 'Is it a small person because the house is so small?' Foreman's props may also proliferate à la Ionesco, but without triggering the nausea and/or violence of the French Absurdist.

All these scenic intricacies replace story intricacies, and through them runs a dialogue which is only sporadically communicative, composed of flat dry words that the characters mouth in flat dry tones. A description by Richard Schechner in *The Village Voice* conveys the effect:

A narrow field of vision with forced perspective; the dancers, always women, staring at the audience, forcing each spectator into acknowledging the role of looker; the framing of slices and planes of actions in an effort to isolate and control ('analyze') them; the ironic or authoritarian voice of the director shouting 'cue' or making comments on the action – but always on tape, mediated and removed from the activity going on now; the buzzer-bell-noise-oompah music of the sports event, the combat-as-play.

160

That combat, in plays of the Ontological/Hysteric Theatre, is at once sexual and artistic, for Foreman may jettison dramatic plot, but he thrives on the battle of the sexes, in which woman lures man from his creative destiny.

The corpus of Foreman's Ontological/Hysteric Theatre is so full of repetition that it is hard to see any single piece as a whole: *Sophia = Wisdom* is the title of four plays; other titles introduce repeated puns – *Pain(t), MISrepresentation, Fall-starts*. From play to play the same characters reappear – clumsy Max the writer, his *alter ego* Ben the lover, another *alter ego* Leo, his seductive girlfriend Rhoda, her jealous rivals Hannah and Eleanor, her friends and helpers Ida and Sophia – and they often appear nude. The repetition of framing and punctuating devices is at once familiar and inventive; playing with planes is the stable, unstable ground of Foreman's drama. Although he abjures plots and inveighs against interpretation, his polarities are insistent – man versus woman, garments versus nakedness, mind versus body, writing versus being, words versus things. To keep his 'action at a distance' – a recent title – Foreman glances parodically at painting, literature, film, philosophy, and most recently he makes 'in' jokes at his own expense: 'Text, text, that's what counts. Not music, not ideas, not decor.' 'Oh, my happiness is complete when I can relate the thing that I am seeing to the thing that I am hearing.' 'Subtlety is not perhaps my forte.'

In Foreman's collection of *Plays and Manifestos* critic Kate Davy has listed his performances up to 1976; he closed his loft in 1979, perhaps terminating the Ontological/Hysteric Theatre. It is pointless to apply traditional critical shorthand to this collection, skimming a number of plays to linger on one that is typical or celebrated or fine. I could say, for example, that *Angelface* (1968) introduces Foreman's characters and devices, with Rhoda appearing in wings; that *Total Recall* (1970) is the boast of Ben, who plays mind to Leo's body while Sophia hides under Hannah's nightgown; that *Hotel China* (1971) is at once sexuality and language, cold and fragile under the impact of theatre rocks. *Sophia = Wisdom: Part 3, the Cliffs* (1971) probably exhibits Foreman's greatest control of his theatre idiom; Rhoda and Ben are the naked views of Sophia and Max, with Hannah and Karl performing in trivial everyday relationships; through the inventive manipulation of cliff-boxes and sexually suggestive props, the male–female rivalries emerge sharply in spite of flat acting. Stefan Brecht has extensively analysed *Particle Theory* (1972) as a reply to *Cliffs*. Foreman himself reads *Pandering to the Masses* (1974) as

the relation between knowing and dying to habit and convention; *Rhoda in Potatoland [1974]* on the physical-ity and urge to tumescence of all 'body-things' as they try to swamp mind-things in us; *Book of Splendors [1977]* on the world experienced as pure 'multiplicity' and the mind's effort to steer clearly through, and using, that multiplicity.

Such skimming virtually neglects the content of these plays, but detailed description would be tedious and extensive. Perhaps it would be illuminating to conclude on Foreman's contrast between theatre of the past and his own:

Old paradigm: Universe consists of forces that solidify into units (Gestalts, objects, events) to which we *re-spond*.

162

New paradigm: Universe consists of forces that leave traces which are not fully identifiable consciously, of which we see only residual evidence – and if we respond it is 'error' of responding to what we *project* into those traces.

If you believe 1, your art tries to make something visible, and the life copied by that art is a responding-to-input from the 'world'.

If you believe 2, your (my) art tries to erase things (because they are obstacles) and the life copied by that art is a 'something else' that tries to resonate to inner output.

The work of the Mabou Mines Company, and particularly of Lee Breuer, might fall between the two paradigms. This company's art is certainly a 'something else' taking a myriad of forms 'to resonate to inner input', and their art also deals in unsettling perceptions spatially and temporally, but they deliberately leave the traces, encouraging a projection from the spectators, eliciting an emotional response. Influenced, like Foreman, by Brecht's distancing of the performance, the Mabou Mines do not reject the Stanislavski-based Method of emotional memory. Attuned like Foreman to art movements like Minimalism and Conceptualism, the Mabou Mines never treat actors as objects, but at once as expressive instruments and virtuosos who play on those instruments.

Their principal playwright is Lee Breuer, born, like Foreman, in 1937, but three thousand miles away in Los Angeles. Growing up there means an awareness of Hollywood, and Hollywood *kitsch* sounds parodically in Breuer's work. A university graduate, like Foreman, Breuer was an English major because he thought that a would-be playwright should read omnivorously, but he spent most of his time in the theatre, where he met actress Ruth Maleczech, whom he later married. (Foreman lives with his main actress, Kate Manheim). University trained, immersed in literature, Breuer and Foreman wrote their first plays for more or less commercial outlets – Breuer winning a national award and Foreman having a play optioned for Broadway. As Brecht, then Stein magnetized Foreman, Beckett attracted Breuer, who hitch-hiked from Los Angeles to San Francisco in order to see the Actor's Workshop production of *Waiting for Godot* in 1956. Disappointed at its bareness, he nurtured an opposition attitude toward the drama of the Absurd, wishing to see plays produced in arresting colours, lights, shapes, textures, harmonies; even before Foreman, he was yearning for a *Gesamtkunstwerk*. As Foreman savoured the experiments of underground film-makers, Breuer was on the fringes of the experimental San Francisco Tape Music Center of Morton Subotnik and Pauline Oliveros. He also worked with Ronnie Davis soon after the founding of the San Francisco Mime Troupe for whom he directed parts of the *Caucasian Chalk Circle* to which he invited composers, dancers, visual artists. In that milieu Breuer met actors JoAnne Akalaitis and Bill Raymond, who later helped create the Mabou Mines.

With their taste for the modern European classics, the Breuers left for Europe in 1965 where, to their surprise, they remained five years, meeting the other members of what was to become the Mabou Mines Company. Living on odd jobs, they pursued theatre activities, but Breuer's role shifted from playwright to director – of Brecht and Beckett. Only when they returned to the States did they found the Mabou Mines Company, named after the Nova Scotia town where JoAnne Akalaitis offered them rehearsal space, and where they began to create collective pieces.

Breuer has so far published only three plays – in a single volume *Animations*. By publication date (1979) he regarded these three animations as steps toward a cycle of six Realms which dramatized 'a story of an unenlightened life'. The titles – *The Red Horse Animation* (1970, revised 1972), *The B. Beaver Animation* (1974), and *The Shaggy Dog Animation* (1978) reveal his reliance on the beast fable tradition that is at least as old as Aesop. The titles also suggest modern film technology; an animation conveys an impression of motion through rapid scanning of stills. And of course animation means vivacity. Breuer has enlisted the aid of book designers, and the *Animations* volume is accompanied by photographs of the company productions, but there is no breakdown of the dialogue as spoken by different actors, and there are no scenic directions. The text itself appears in block capital letters, punctuated only by periods. Since the publication dates from 1979, it is too soon to say whether other directors than Breuer will be tempted to enact his words, but it is not too soon to realize that the words make dramatic reading.

Originally played by three actors, *The Red Horse Animation* opens in three printed columns that Breuer calls tracks – Outline, Lifeline, Storyline. Some third of the way through the piece, however, Lifeline and Storyline merge. The three columns begin with avatars of the same question: 'Why pretend?' or 'Why make art?' The script is its own nebulous answer, whose movement is a rising action, a culmination, and a rather swift fall. The Outline, as is fitting, worries about form and shape; the Lifeline veers from the physical lifeline in the palm of a hand to the metaphysical line of spiritlife; the Storyline blends an American boyhood with a romantic dream of red horses crossing the Gobi Desert in the time of Genghis Khan. Each red horse bears a message wrapped around an arrow;

he is driven to the limit of endurance before the message is transferred to another horse. When Lifeline and Storyline join, to the punctuation of cinematic cuts and pans, the horse wonders about the message, and the text closes in on one such horse, quoting Beckett: 'HOW I HOLD ME IN MY ARMS AND TELL ME A STORY.'

Much of the story is about the red horse's sire, Daily Bread, fitted with blinkers, tied to a pole, and compelled to circle endlessly on the thresher floor – 'A HORSE'S ASS'. Docile and traditional, Daily Bread (a pun on money and the staff of life) meditates on what he will eventually say, but the cord around his neck cracks his windpipe, so that his words are incomprehensible to his son. The Outline then turns to the red horse whose Life- and Storylines are a continuous *line*, in reaction against the circles of Daily Bread, the humdrum sire. With illness, the red horse sees himself as mere representation; the figure of a red horse can no longer contain him; he cannot find himself through a romance, and Outline concludes: 'YOU. LOSE. IT.' Condensed, witty, subtly rhythmed, the play plunges an equine metaphor into the surround of modern electronic and cinematic technology, to create the portrait of the artist as a young theatre.

B. Beaver is a very different animal, accompanied in performance by his family, but the actors are also objects and natural forces. Busy as his proverbial ancestor, B. Beaver tells his own story in the wider of two printed columns. The other erupts in occasional sardonic commentary or scenic directions. Breuer labels them TEXT and TAKES – again the cinematic vocabulary. The red horse reacts against the life style of his sire, but B. Beaver rages against the elements that threaten his dam (a three-way pun), in which he takes possessive pride: 'THE WORLD'S

FINEST BLEND OF CHOICE SILTS ORGANIC COMPOST EARTHY ALKALIS FRESH BROOK SHALE NOT TO MENTION LABOR.' Persisting in fiction, he is another Breuer artist and also a pedantic pedagogue to his brood. *His* daily fiction runs to natural forces which he analyses with the help of an alphabet of nonsense algebra. Panicking in spring, he writes for do-it-yourself help on his dam: 'I AM A BEAVER WHO HAS LOST THE ART OF DAMNATION AT A CRUCIAL TIME.' But there is no reply. Confused but reasoning like Beckett's Unnamable, he puns in sorrow at the rush of spring: 'GET ON TOP OF WHAT'S UP. GET RIGHT TO THE BOTTOM OF WHAT'S GOING DOWN.' He battles with a trout in an extended prize-fight conceit. He wins, with assistance from the *Book of Job*. Busier and busier, he plans and studies; he is an example of 'A SPECIES IN EXTREMITIES'.

B. Beaver struggles on to protect his dam, and he has at his disposal an arsenal of modern slang and puns, the vocabularies of geology, zoology, boxing; a few dashes of Latin and a few more of Beckett. Like Beckett's intellectuals, he marshals reason and reading to stave off chaos. In vain. After the dam bursts, a letter arrives with no information but numbers, and he answers in kind. The last sardonic comment informs us that B. Beaver ends up as a Wino on Second Avenue. As the red horse sought form, B. Beaver wanted to strengthen his dam, and Breuer's wit dramatizes his damnation. But it is never mere wit, since the verbal force explodes the set (literally) to dramatize the vanity of trying to dam the melting snows of spring, the vanity of an artist trying to dam his medium.

Most ambitious of Breuer's animations is *The Shaggy Dog*, about four times as long as either of the others, some four hours in the Mabou Mines performance, involving eight actors and a puppet. The text as published bifurcates into Sound and Image Tracks, and it too uses a beast fable (even though a shaggy dog is a fictitious beast) to dramatize the life of the artist, in three parts. On the page the Sound Track, a broad column in Breuer's customary capital letters, takes epistolary form. The letters begin: 'Dear John', the euphemism of the Second World War for the letter that told a soldier he was being replaced with another lover. These Dear John letters, however, are addressed to movie cameraman John Greed by Rose-Shaggy Dog-puppet-movie cutter; in performance, the letters are spoken by several actors, but the printed text does not designate these divisions.

The opening Sound Track informs us that Rose, having left John, is writing him a letter that flashes back to their meeting, to her puppy love for him, and to her rivalry with 'that female person' Leslie. The Image Track in contrast, is never epistolary, but descriptive, sardonic, meditative in self-address by Rose. The Sound Track letter recalls that Leslie, an actress on location in Venice, California, sent John an airplane ticket with instructions to come without the dog, but he takes his faithful hound. On the beach John and Rose dropped acid and knew a night of rapture. Even in recollection on the Sound Track, Rose shifts to the future tense as they become one species: 'YOUR SKIN WILL ASK FOR ME. AS MY EYE ASKS TO LOOK AT YOU. AND EACH TO EACH OTHER. WILL BE REVEALED.' But the Image Track reduces the love scene to camera specifics, and Part I ends in a rush of contemporary sitcom clichés about lovers parting.

In Part II they have separated, and we follow Rose. While the Image Track hides Rose's misery in recipes, the Sound Track delivers a history of dogs as domesticated animals. The Sound Track then recounts Rose's affair with Bunny, but on the Image Track she talks movie language with Ed. Her affair with Bunny ends in Las Vegas, and back in New York City she surprises herself with a litter by the dog Broadway. Having to make a living, Rose enters the art world: 'I LEARNED TO SHAKE HANDS. PLAY DEAD. AND BEG. TWO WEEKS LATER I PICKED UP A CAPS GRANT . . . . SPEAKING PUBLICLY I PICKED UP A BARK WORSE THAN MY BITE.' In a hilarious parody of critical jargon, Rose retires from the art market. She tries to recapture her life with John, but then questions whether it is fit material for a movie: 'WAS I A DOG. OR A COPYCAT.' She flashes back to their last ferocious communication when they flung identical insults at one another. Near a garbage truck they again take leave of one another, to end Part II.

In Part III Rose reads about John's offer of a reward for a lost dog, with a three-year-old picture of her. She has her own life on the Sound Track; on the Image Track John as puppet at first speaks to two different people on two different phones, but soon he narrows down to himself as professional movie-maker talking shop, and through it revealing his artistic desperation. Ending without ending the telephone conversation, the play reverts to the Sound Track – first a recitation of clichés about trying to renounce an obsessive habit, and then a retreat into the unconscious for the dog–artist–lover who should know better but doesn't. Finally, rhymingly, Rose declares her independence: 'JACK SMACK. I HEAR YOU KNOCKING. BUT YOU CAN'T COME IN. SING ME A CHORUS OF CHERRY PIE. WRONG LIFE BABY. NEXT TIME. MAYBE. I TELL YOU THE TRUTH. ONLY SLEEPING DOGS LIE.' And sleeping is not for hyperactive shaggy dog Rose, who has plunged us in truths through her tracks.

New York critic Bonnie Marranca has grouped Breuer with Foreman (and many other avant-garde artists) as Theatre of Images, a phrase that seems to me too inclusive; all theatre contains images, but images do not necessarily build theatre. More acute is her isolation of several

characteristics that these playwrights share – tableau as unit
of composition, sophisticated aural technology, substitu-
tion of inner monologue for dialogue. Moreover, both
Foreman and Breuer take art as subject, and neither
playwright-director jettisons *both* plot *and* character.
Breuer weaves a story through his intricate actions, and
Foreman imprisons his characters in myriad scenic activities. Granted that the printed plays reveal much less than
traditional playscripts about the perceptual complexities of
performance. Nevertheless, these playwrights have offered
their texts for public perusal, and newer-wave theatre
practitioners may visualize and concretize them in ways as
yet unimagined.

10
The Word is my Shepard

Sam Shepard has written enduring drama, which is a fitting finale for this overview of two decades. Produced Off-Off-Broadway at the age of nineteen, published and winning an Obie at twenty-three, contracted to write a movie at twenty-five, subsidized at Lincoln Center at twenty-seven, contracted to act in a movie – for a six-figure sum – at thirty-five, admired by academics as well as rock fans, Sam Shepard would seem to be fortune's child. With some forty plays written, he has moved from early images of fragmentation to sustained theatre metaphors of a moribund civilization – our own. His recent plays are cast in the tragic shadow of Eugene O'Neill, and he resembles O'Neill, too, in gravitating from experimental to more realistic forms.

Born on a midwestern Army base in 1943, growing up mainly on a California ranch, arriving in New York City in the 1960s, living for three years in London, he has various landscapes at his disposal. Bored at school, gifted in timpani, devoted to sports, Shepard naturally thinks in terms of popular rather than pedantic myths. In the loose

Bohemianism of Greenwich Village in the 1960s, he tried his hand at song lyrics, brief vignettes, and short plays. Three Obies in swift succession fixed his genre. (He now has seven Obies.) These early plays may change locale – indoors, outdoors, home, or hotel – but the time is always now. In form, associative monologues are glued on to disjunctive exchanges; collage is an apt description.

Cowboys and *Rock Garden* (1964) were produced on a double bill at Off-Off-Broadway Theatre Genesis, and they carry themes and images that recur in Shepard's work. He has explained *Cowboys*:

> Cowboys are really interesting to me – these guys, most of them really young, about 16 to 17, who decided they didn't want to have anything to do with the East Coast . . . and took on that immense country, and didn't have any real rules . . . . I wrote the original *Cowboys,* and then I rewrote it and called it No 2, and that's all. The original is lost now.

We can sketch Shepard from this comment: dedicated to Western legend; careless of his own scripts; admiring of figures who 'didn't have any real rules' – not only cowboys, but rock stars, sports champions, drug visionaries, young men rebelling against family constraint. The quotation also suggests that Shepard may not be the most acute critic of his own plays.

Cowboys #2, a rewriting of his first play, does not dramatize the young outlaws he praises, but two young men in an unlocalized setting, who nourish their imaginations on cowboys. Throughout the brief play they alternate between their reality as young men in a contemporary city and roles as old cowboys from scenes of film Westerns. In their inevitable battle with Indians, the audience sees a construction saw-horse and hears the offstage sound of galloping horses – an audio-visual pun. Only as cowboy comrades do the two men achieve communion. In contrast, their contemporary reality imposes isolation, and each young man delivers a manic monologue – a device that will become Shepard's trademark. At the play's end they enact old cowboys threatened by blazing sun and vultures; they are joined on stage (but not in communication) by two other young men in business suits, with scripts from which they monotonously read the opening lines of the play. Whereas the original two men are nourished by the popular cowboy myth, their contemporaries are locked into dull practicalities. It is not mere language but vivid enactment that can create cowboys on a bare stage, which is Shepard's version of two boards and a passion – a passion for pop images. This re-creation of his first play blends rule-free cowboys and carefree artists. Outside myth, however, in contemporary urban reality, monologues turn sour on the tongue.

In actual fact, a monologue from Shepard's first extant play brought him a first taste of success, when it was bought by Kenneth Tynan for *Oh! Calcutta.* Shepard's play is more exciting than Tynan's. *Rock Garden* (1964) dramatizes mutual incomprehension within a family – a theme that recurs over a decade later in Shepard's realistic trilogy. In *Rock Garden* an adolescent boy threads through three scenes in three rooms of a house. Scene 1 is silent as the boy and his sister sip milk, unnoticed by their father reading a magazine. In Scene 2 the boy in underwear in a rocking chair asks laconic, sometimes insidious questions of a garrulous woman in her bed. Three times she likens one of the boy's features to his father's or grandfather's, and each time he returns from an errand with clothing over the inherited feature. At the end of the scene the man in underwear replaces the boy, and the woman is reduced to monosyllables. In Scene 3 father and son are both in underwear in their living room. Like the woman in the second scene the man speaks a virtual monologue, punctuated only by the boy's laconic, insidious questions and occasional falls from his chair. The father airs a fantasy about a rock garden, and, after a long pause, the son spews forth a monologue about sexual pleasure, which knocks the man off his couch. A contemporary *Spring's Awakening*, the play ends on a verbal climax about sexual climax. Father and son project wholly separate rock gardens. (Rocks are slang for testicles, as Richard Foreman also realizes.) In Scene 1 the father is oblivious to the sexual stirrings of his children. In Scene 2 the mother is oblivious to sexual implications of her remarks on heredity and temperature. Finally, stripped to underwear, father and son engage in a dialogue of the deaf. Man, woman, and boy sing the same refrains: 'I don't know . . . . You know?' without knowing one another.

This example of generation gap is unusual in Shepard's early collages, which revolve about people his own age. In his first two years as a playwright Shepard dramatizes his contemporaries in telling caricatures of American reality. On simple but striking stage sets, young men and women act compulsively, without making conventional sense. Shepard's young people flex their lexical muscles in long arias. Inventive, associative, syntactically simple but image-laden, the monologues are often paced by a refrain. Although these monologues resemble traditional soliloquies in exploring the speaker's inner life, that life bears obliquely on the minimal plots of the collages. Critic Frances Rademacher compares them to Pinter's plays, in which words are weapons in a territorial imperative.

A second group of plays begins with *La Turista* (1967)

although Shepard also continues to write a few residual collages. In this main group, which may be labelled fantasy (but freer and deeper than those of McClure) fantastic or mythic characters figure in sustained plots, surcharged with incident. In *La Turista* pop and ritual elements are blended and force-fed into a classic structure of plague and catharsis. A more probable blend is that of pop music and crime in *Melodrama Play* (1967). *Forensic and the Navigators* (1967) can barely contain its mixture of science fiction, political revolution, and satirized bureaucracy.

Although *La Turista* (written in Mexico under the influence of amphetamines and dysentery) is one of Shepard's first plays to sustain a plot; that plot is not linear since the second act precedes the first chronologically, but parallels it formally. Shepard's title puns on the Spanish word for 'tourist' and the diarrhoea that afflicts tourists in Mexico. In a brightly coloured Mexican hotel room an American couple, Kent and Salem, suffer from this illness and severe sunburn. A native shoe-shine boy also irritates them, and when Kent faints, Salem telephones for a doctor. Enter a witch-doctor and son who engage in an arcane ceremony that lasts throughout the act. The shoe-shine boy translates their ritual for the *turistas,* dons Kent's cowboy costume, and is auctioned off before being wooed by Salem to return to the States with her. At the end of Act I Kent lies inert before the chanting witch-doctor and his son. Act II finds Kent and Salem again in a hotel room, but this one sports American plastic. Kent is ill with sleeping sickness, behaving as if in a trance. This time Salem's S.O.S. brings a father–son team behaving like country doctors of Western films, replete with drawl. On Doc's order, Salem and his son (played by the shoe-shine boy of Act I) keep Kent walking, but the drama gradually narrows down to a verbal duel between Doc and Kent.

175

In a face-off where Doc uses a real gun and Kent an imaginary one, the two men circle one another, Kent verbally transforming into a hunted monster. Suiting action to description, Kent leaps off the stage and runs behind the audience, where he assumes a dual role of prey and hunter. Moreover, the two antagonists exchange roles: 'Doc gets through different gestures that were Kent's in the first act', and Kent portrays a doctor merging with his victim: 'Doc must get there first and escape with the beast.' Doc on stage shouts for Salem and his son to capture Kent, and the latter pursues his account of the doctor–hunter emotionally tied to his patient–victim. After this verbal barrage, the play's end is strikingly gestural; Kent eludes Salem and Sonny by swinging Tarzan-like over the heads of the audience and on to the stage. He then 'runs straight toward the upstage wall of the set and leaps right through it, leaving a cut-out silhouette of his body in the wall.'

The names of Kent and Salem, well-known brands of American cigarettes, suggest an indictment of contemporary America – a theme that recurs in Shepard's plays. Tourists abroad and in their own country, Kent and Salem suffer in Act I from the food and climate of Mexico, but they cannot be cured by that country's rituals, to which they feel superior. At home in the United States, however, suffering from sleeping sickness, Kent cannot be cured by an outworn popular model of his own country. In both acts the father–son doctors are rooted in their own cultural ground, which proves to be quicksand for a contemporary American. By the play's end, Kent is apparently cured of illness through his pop culture roles – Macho cowboy in Act I, and in Act II gangster, monster, hunter, Tarzan – and an extraordinary verbal imagination.

Kent seems to be a professional tourist in *La Turista,* but *Melodrama Play* (1967), written a few weeks later, dramatizes the artist as a young musician. As *La Turista* reflects cowboy and monster films, *Melodrama Play* reflects gangster films and the rock music scene of the 1960s. The stage is dominated by large eyeless photographs of Bob Dylan, king of rock, and Robert Goulet, king of crooners. Rock star Duke Durgens wears 'extra long hair, shades, jeans, boots, vest, etc', as do Duke's brother Drake, his friend Cisco, and four members of a rock band present throughout the play.

Having composed a hit song, Duke is coerced by his manager Floyd to compose another hit, as Shepard's Horse-dreamer will be coerced in *Geography of a Horse-Dreamer* to name a winner, as his Rabbit Brown will be coerced to create a hit disaster movie in *Angel City,* but his composer Niles will flee coercion in *Suicide in B Flat.* Actually, Drake composed the hit song of *Melodrama Play,* which his brother Duke then recorded and sold to Floyd. Ordering his girlfriend Dana to cut his hair, Duke moves from the Dylan to the Goulet image, whereupon Floyd orders his strongman Peter to guard Duke, Drake, Dana, and Cisco until a song hit is produced, no matter who composes it. With melodramatic violence, Peter shoots Dana, knocks Duke and Cisco unconscious, and bars Floyd from the room. While Peter plays cat-and-mouse with the true composer Drake, Duke on the radio sings the hit song: 'So prisoners, get up out a' your homemade beds.' One by one, Duke, Cisco, and Dana rise from the floor and leave the stage, since this is a melodrama *play*. Yet the final image is not playful. As Peter raises his club against the composer Drake, there is a knock on the door. Commerce knocking outside, thug bludgeoning inside – that is the precarious, melodramatic position of the artist.

Of the three fantasies written in 1967, *Forensic and the Navigators* is fuzziest as to plot and character. It was, however, the occasion for Shepard's meeting his wife O-Lan who gave her name to her role. She changes in the play from someone enslaved to two revolutionaries into an object of desire for an exterminator of revolutionaries. In an ending that explodes from nowhere the whole setting goes up in smoke. Perhaps Shepard himself sensed the play's weakness since it was followed by a two-year silence – the most extended of his career.

By 1970 a play was commissioned from Shepard (by Jules Irving) for the Vivian Beaumont Theatre of New York's Lincoln Center. *Operation Sidewinder* resembles earlier Shepard plays in its titular pun; the sidewinder is both rattlesnake and military computer. Its intricate spectacular plot has been succinctly summarized by critic John Lahr: 'A six-foot sidewinder, which is really an escaped military computer; black, white, and Indian renegades plotting to capture Air Force planes by putting dope in a military reservoir; a Hopi snake dance whose ritual transforms the sidewinder computer from military property to religious icon.' Winding through this labyrinthine intrigue is a handsome young couple – an aimless hippy and a honey-haired *ingénue*. Lifted from the tale of Indian Geronimo is half-breed Mickey Free, who first rescues Honey from the sidewinder and then welcomes the young couple to the concluding Indian ceremony. The grand finale resembles a Disneyland version of New Comedy – boy gets girl against a fantasmagoria of costumed dances, billowing breezes, and coloured lights.

Shepard also ends *Mad Dog Blues* (1971) on song and dance, but it is a revel *ex machina*. Apparently written in a drugged state, the 'two-act adventure show' manipulates nine characters dear to an undrugged Shepard. The cowboy figure, Waco Texas, is joined by a rock star Kosmo, a drug addict Yahoudi, and popular figures of fact and fiction. On a bare stage these characters travel far and wide, through ocean and desert, within an island and across a frontier, past one another though they are close enough to touch. Two friends, Kosmo the rock star who 'leads with his cock' and Yahoudi the drug addict who 'sucks in the printed word' separately leave New York City. In Frisco Kosmo conjures up Mae West, and in a vision Yahoudi finds Marlene Dietrich. Kosmo then collects cowboy Waco Texas while Yahoudi joins up with Captain Kidd of the legendary treasure. All characters go hunting for the treasure, and they tumble through swift adventures redolent of films. Marlene leaves Yahoudi for Paul Bunyan, lonely without his blue ox Babe.

Act II opens on Yahoudi's threats to Captain Kidd, echoing *The Treasure of the Sierra Madre*. As fast as film cuts, characters journey around the stage's treasure island. Yahoudi shoots Captain Kidd and then himself, falling on the treasure, where Kosmo and Mae discover him. Soon Jesse James robs Kosmo of treasure and Mae. Kosmo implores his friend Yahoudi to return to life and help him manoeuvre the other characters. In vain. Each character is locked in his own myth, but they nevertheless 'keep searching for each other but never meet, even though at times THEY may pass right by each other.' Only Jesse James and Mae West travel together, with bags full of treasure. On Paul Bunyan's ox, they stampede across the border into the United States. When the treasure turns out to be bottle-caps, Jesse James heads home for Missouri, to which Mae invites all the others, including a resurrected Yahoudi. The play closes on an improbable celebration – the last of Shepard's plays to do so.

Only a month after *Mad Dog Blues* Shepard dramatized blues again, in a musician who dreaded becoming a rock star. *Cowboy Mouth,* written in collaboration with Patti

Smith, and first enacted by Shepard and Smith, is inevitably read biographically, but the play's drive and intensity belie the rumour of the play's origin in the two principals pushing a typewriter back and forth across a table. A woman Cavale has kidnapped Slim from his wife and child in order to fashion him into a rock messiah: 'You gotta be like a rock-and-roll Jesus with a cowboy mouth.' In her studio littered with symbolic debris (notably a dead crow) the couple alternately quarrel, play scenes, play music, reminisce, and order food which a scarlet-shelled Lobsterman delivers. Cavale fascinates Slim with her tales of French outlaw artists – Villon, Genet and Nerval who walked through Paris with a lobster on a leash. The couple again send for the Lobsterman who sheds his red carapace when they begin to sing. Looking like a rock messiah, the ex-Lobsterman is given a gun by departing Slim. As the silent Lobsterman spins its chambers, Cavale tells *him* about Nerval who had a pet lobster and hanged himself on her birthday, whence her name Cavale or 'escape'.

Brilliantly theatrical, the play implicitly denies its title. The masses may 'want a saint . . . with a cowboy mouth. Somebody to get off on when they can't get off on themselves.' But Slim retreats from that demand, and the very name of Cavale means escape. Although the Lobsterman strikes an empty chamber to end the play, the possibility is always there that artists may die young, but they cannot be saviours. A cowboy mouth or a lobster shell – neither one heralds a messiah.

Melodrama Play, Mad Dog Blues, Cowboy Mouth are stages of preparation for Shepard's most incisive portrait of an artist, *The Tooth of Crime,* written in England in 1972. The title comes from a sonnet by Mallarmé, read to Shepard by Patti Smith. The French line translates: 'A heart that the tooth of crime cannot wound.' Mallarmé's sonnet contrasts a vulnerable persona with his invulnerable partner in vice, and Shepard's play contrasts vulnerable Hoss with invulnerable Crow. Like classical tragedy, *The Tooth of Crime* begins close to its climax: Hoss needs a kill. He fondles an array of weapons displayed by Becky, his servant, mistress, and tutor. Wiser than Shakespeare's Caesar who ignored the stars, Hoss consults his Star-Man and is advised against moving. Wiser than Shakespeare's Richard II, he seeks counsel from Galactic Jack who reassures him: 'A shootin' star, baby, High flyin' and no jivin'. You is off to number nine.' But Hoss is not reassured and is almost relieved when his fear takes human shape. Becky reports that a Gypsy has been 'sussed' – Shepard's polyvalent borrowing from Cockney slang. Hoss sounds out his chauffeur Cheyenne about cruising, but this faithful retainer is reluctant to violate the code. Lacking support, Hoss seeks an ally in the East but learns of his suicide. Distraught, Hoss sends for the Doc to give him an injection, but he is not tranquillized. Warned against cruising, Hoss nevertheless is somewhat soothed by Becky's cruising song. Hoss stalks and knifes a dummy, then recalls the camaraderie of his youth. Alone on stage, he engages in an imaginary dialogue with his father: 'They're all countin' on me. The bookies, the agents, the Keepers. I'm a fucking industry.' Hoss speaks his father's reply: 'You're just a man, Hoss. Just a man.' Having accepted that limitation, Hoss awaits Crow. Weary, enthroned under a huge shadow of Crow, Hoss absorbs Crow's song 'Poison' to close Act I.

Act II opens with Crow along on stage, dressed in the hard rock style of the 1960s. As Shakespeare's Prince Hal tried on his father's crown, Crow sits in Hoss's throne-like chair. When Hoss arrives, Crow addresses him in clipped metaphors: 'Got the molar chomps. Eyes stitched. You can vision what's sittin'. Very razor to cop z's sussin' me to be on the far end of the spectrum.' From his royal isolation, Hoss asks Crow for news of the outside world, then orders him off the throne and summons a referee to judge their agon. In Round 1 Crow attacks Hoss with a capsule biography of a coward. Ref awards the round to Crow. In Round 2 Hoss accuses Crow of denying his musical origins in the blues of the Blacks, but Crow counters: 'I'm in a different time.' The Ref declares it a draw. In Round 3 Crow ridicules Hoss's outdated music, and the Ref calls it a technical knockout. An infuriated Hoss shoots the Ref, thereby becoming a gypsy outside law.

Hoss turns to Crow for instructions in survival. In a digression imitating the film *Alphaville* Becky enacts a seduction of her youth, with Hoss perhaps the aggressor. Hoss himself cannot learn to talk, walk, and sing like a gypsy. Like classical heroes, he prefers death to dishonour:

> Now stand back and watch some true style. The mark of a lifetime. A true gesture that won't never cheat on itself 'cause it's the last of its kind. It can't be taught or copied or stolen or sold. It's mine. An original. It is my life and my death in one clean shot.

Hoss falls upon that shot, and Crow pays him homage: 'A genius mark'. Crow's reign begins, and his final song is a prayer for supremacy, like Hoss's plea to his advisers at the play's beginning.

Embracing earlier Shepard themes – swiftly changing modes of art, mechanization of popular culture, the artist who dies mid-career, the messianic hope of rock music, even a hint of father-son relations – *Tooth* explores American culture. Through highly imaged, rhythmic monologues and through duelling dialogues, Hoss and

Crow reveal themselves intimately, and through them we gain insight into a contemporary cacophony of big business, crime, sports, astrology, art.

Shepard again dramatizes the artist in *Angel City* and *Suicide in B Flat* (1976). The Angel City artist is Rabbit Brown, shabbily dressed, travelling by buckboard, tied to magic bundles. He is invited to Angel City to invent a disaster that will create a movie triumph. The Suicide artist is jazz composer Niles, who is the titular suicide or victim of murder. By the end of *Angel City* Rabbit is fanged and long-nailed, oozing green slime; he has metamorphosed into the mogul who summoned him. The B flat musician has responded to pressure by repeating himself artistically; in order to escape to his own original music, he has to simulate his own death. At first invisible to musicians and detectives, he is finally apprehended and handcuffed.

In 1976, the year of these satiric fantasies, Shepard also turned to realism. He had already confessed in 1974: 'I'd like to try a whole different way of writing now, which is very stark and not so flashy and not full of a lot of mythic figures and everything, and try to scrape it down to the bone as much as possible.' The repetition of 'try' may hint that Shepard is working against the grain, but it is nevertheless a grain that has brought him fame, with fortune seeping through his film roles.

Hardly stark and still mythic, *Curse of the Starving Class* (1976), *Buried Child* (1978) and *True West* (1980) are realistic in setting, straightfoward in plot, and coherent in character. The plays have been called American Gothic, and they may also be Shepard's attempts at Greek tragedy. He himself speaks of them as a 'family trilogy'. The starving class is a Western family on an avocado farm with some cattle; the child is buried on a midwestern farm gone to seed. Both Western and midwestern families are cursed, even as the House of Atreus. In *Starving Class* the curse is literally Emma's first menstrual period, and the figurative family inheritance: 'We inherit /the curse/ and pass it down, and then pass it down again. It goes on and on like that without us.' The very names announce a hereditary curse: father Weston and son Wesley, mother Ella and daughter Emma – the same names, except for a letter or two. Although the family members claim not to belong to the starving class, they do, starving for identity and dignity. Every family member keeps opening and closing the refrigerator door. Middle-class Americans, the family is so debt-cursed that their home is prey to predators. Only son Wesley understands the magnitude of that curse: 'So it means more than losing a house. It means losing a country.' At the end of the play, mother and son recite a parable of the cat and the eagle, clawing at one another high in the air: 'And they come crashing down to earth. Both of them come crashing down. Like one whole thing.' Greedy America has seized its own killer, a domestic animal driven berserk far from its natural environment.

Neither parable nor imaginative monologue relieves the lower depths of midwestern farm life in *Buried Child*. Grandfather Dodge is a sedentary cougher solaced only by televison and whiskey. Grandmother Halie in Whistlerian black flirts with a clergyman to promote a statue for her dead son. More or less alive are her sons Tilden, an ex-football star and present half-wit, and Bradley, a sadistic cripple before whom the others cower. Home to the family bosom come grandson musician Vince and his California girlfriend. Appalled though he is by this return to his roots, Vince decides to remain and face his dubious heritage. His father Tilden, having dug up carrots and corn from the backyard, ends the play carrying the decayed corpse of a buried child. Realistically, Dodge has murdered his wife's probably incestuous infant, but symbolically youth is buried by the American family – incestuous, idiotic, sadistic, and moribund.

In *True West* two brothers, Ivy League Austin and ne'er-do-well Lee, compete in composing a movie scenario about the true West. With neither parable nor monologue, the play's first act contains the most pointed humour Shepard has written – familial, social, Western American. But Act II belabours the weary Western motif, in determined full-evening realism. Shepard needs Chaikin to call again to collaborate as in *Tongues* (1978/9), releasing his unique imagery.

Since winning the Pulitzer Prize, Shepard has suffered easy reduction by critics; one sees him obsessed by father–son conflicts, another by quests that end at home, a third by escape from American materialism into an interior life. It is not, however, theme but image and rhythm that render Shepard's plays memorable – some of them. Often starting with an image, he then casts characters around it, and only then conceives events: 'I'm taking notes in as much detail as possible on an event that's happening somewhere inside me.' It is this detail that magnetizes audiences to these events. Every Shepard critic has described the hypnotic quality of his monologues, but more pertinent is the way Shepard has learned to subdue these tirades to the dramatic exigencies of the particular play. Collage, fantasy, and the recent larger-than-life tragic realism – the best plays in each of these modes startle the eye, haunt the ear, tickle the funny-bone, and etch a deep impression on the mind.

Shepard has been hailed as the all-American playwright, as though there were a virtue in speaking for a chosen people. Like his ancestor O'Neill, however, Shepard in maturity is dramatizing a tragic America, mired in sin. Like

185

Fitzgerald of *The Great Gatsby,* Shepard is at once
educed by and critical of American wealth and its arte-
facts. Like Thomas Wolfe, he realizes that you can't go
home again – to a pastoral civilization. Like no other
American playwright, Shepard enfolds figures of popular
culture into more lasting patterns of myth – true West, rock
stars, detectives, science fiction. It was by chance that this
Westerner by temperament found himself in New York's
East Village in the mid-1960s. 'It was incredible luck', he
has said, 'to be around when something like Off-Off-
Broadway was getting off the ground. But the 1960s were
kinda awful. I don't even want to think about it.'